Advance Praise
for
Leadership in Balance

"Kucia and Gravett's *Leadership in Balance* describes the shifting concepts of leadership that have given organizations the power to be more collaborative in the way they work, as well as in the ways they are learning to trust the creativity of their own people. For academic institutions in particular, *Leadership in Balance* offers a welcome alternative to the administrative practices that too often have encouraged professors to see themselves as independent contractors."
—Robert Zemsky, Professor and Chair, The Learning Alliance,
University of Pennsylvania, USA

"Heightened demands on organizations of all kinds for increased accountability, transparency, and responsiveness require leaders who understand that collaboration and the deliberate building of trust and commitment among key stakeholders is tantamount to success. Building on insights and observations from a broad base of academic knowledge and practical experience, Kucia and Gravett present a thoughtful and workable leadership framework suited for the dynamic operating environment that characterizes the twenty-first century."
—John C. Lechleiter, Chairman, President, and CEO,
Eli Lilly and Company

"*Leadership in Balance* overflows with ideas that challenge business and government leaders to examine their own thinking and adopt new ways of perceiving their own place in their organizations. Kucia and Gravett present cutting-edge principles that combine Eastern and Western cultural styles, creating a genuine balanced style that anyone in a position of influence can use to deal more effectively with both peers and subordinates. Each chapter engages and motivates the reader to proceed onward with intense anticipation for gaining deeper leadership insights and ideas to be shared with colleagues."
—Robert E. Wubbolding, Professor Emeritus, Xavier University,
USA; Director of Training, The William Glasser Institute
(1988–2011); Director, Center for Reality Therapy,
Cincinnati, USA

"Kucia and Gravett provide an important evolution in leadership literature. Drawing on interviews with CEOs of major corporations and nonprofit organizations, the authors develop a 'balance framework' that replaces hierarchical management with a leadership style that blends and orchestrates competing organizational dimensions, such as competition versus collaboration, in accordance with the organization's mission, structure, and culture. The resulting balance leverages the benefits of each dimension to increase organizational effectiveness."

—Joe Pichler, retired CEO and Chairman,
The Kroger Company

"A must read for all leaders and 'wanna-be' leaders. Unlike the typical treatise on leadership, *Leadership in Balance: New Habits of the Mind* provides a profound glimpse at the inner experiences of today's successful leaders. The emphasis on 'a deeper dimension' of leadership is not only theoretically based, but also measurable, with both ample anecdotal and promising empirical support. Professors, workshop trainers, and inquisitive researchers who focus on leadership should include this book in their 'toolbox for learning.'"

—David T. Hellkamp, Professor Emeritus, Xavier University,
USA; Past-President, Society of Consulting Psychologists,
American Psychological Association

"The twenty-first-century business landscape is turning out to be complex, volatile, and often uncertain. Leadership charlatans would have us believe that we can navigate such landscapes with a few simple management tricks. Kucia and Gravett have instead wisely offered us a more thoughtful, balanced vision of the leader's role."

—Chris Lowney, author, *Heroic Leadership* and *Pope Francis:
Why He Leads the Way He Leads*

Leadership in Balance

New Habits of the Mind

John F. Kucia and Linda S. Gravett

LEADERSHIP IN BALANCE

First published in 2014 by
PALGRAVE MACMILLAN®
in the United States—a division of St. Martin's Press LLC,
175 Fifth Avenue, New York, NY 10010.

Where this book is distributed in the UK, Europe and the rest of the world,
this is by Palgrave Macmillan, a division of Macmillan Publishers Limited,
registered in England, company number 785998, of Houndmills,
Basingstoke, Hampshire RG21 6XS.

Palgrave Macmillan is the global academic imprint of the above companies
and has companies and representatives throughout the world.

Palgrave® and Macmillan® are registered trademarks in the United States,
the United Kingdom, Europe and other countries.

ISBN: 978–1–137–39433–0

Library of Congress Cataloging-in-Publication Data is available from the
Library of Congress.

A catalogue record of the book is available from the British Library.

Design by Newgen Knowledge Works (P) Ltd., Chennai, India.

First edition: April 2014

D 10 9 8 7 6 5 4 3 2

Contents

List of Illustrations   vii

Acknowledgments   ix

Introduction
Leadership in Balance: New Habits of the Mind   xi

Part I   Building the Fundamentals

Chapter 1
Leader as Brand   3

Chapter 2
A New Model of Leadership for a Living
Organization   15

Chapter 3
It's Time for a Different Leadership Paradigm   23

Chapter 4
The Structure of the Ways of Leaders in Balance   45

Chapter 5
The Power of Leadership in Balance: The
Connection to an Organization's Survival   63

Chapter 6
New Habits of the Mind: The Ways of a Leader
in Balance   73

Part II What Does It All Mean—Taking
It to the Next Level

Chapter 7
New Behaviors That Correlate to The Eight Ways
of Thinking   87

Chapter 8
The Kucia Balance Framework in Action   105

Chapter 9
Learning from Mentors through The Eight Ways
of Thinking   117

Chapter 10
The Research Foundation for Leadership in Balance   143

Chapter 11
The Fundamental Shift: Capstone Thoughts   149

Appendix 1
Self-Assessment: A Leader in Balance—The Eight
Ways of Thinking   155

Appendix 2
Self-Assessment: A Leader in Balance—Short Form   157

Appendix 3
ANOVA Results   159

Notes   163

Index   169

About the Authors   177

Chapter 7

Illustrations

Figures

3.1 Balanced leadership thinking positively leverages
human capital 32

3.2 Balanced leadership thinking impacts human
capital success 35

3.3 The PACE of change 41

4.1 Kanji for collaboration—flip chart 48

4.2 The Collaboration Equation 49

4.3 The DNA of Collaboration: The Kucia Balance
Framework 53

4.4 The DNA ladder 57

4.5 The classic double helix twisted 58

4.6 A closer view of interdependence—Yin and Yang 59

5.1 Trust Audit: Do you have a high-trust
organization? 65

5.2 Balancing tradition with potential 68

5.3 Model for Resiliency 70

7.1 Stages along the diversity continuum 99

8.1 Communications Model 109

8.2 The PACE of change and leadership in balance 113

9.1 Leader in balance 119

11.1 Human systems 153

Tables

10.1 Correlations between eight dimensions on
short and long form assessments 146

A3.1   Overall means and standard deviations for the
       long- and short-form dimensions   159
A3.2   Correlations among all dimensions and total
       scores between the two forms   160
A3.3   One-way between-subjects ANOVA results for
       the short-form and the long-form total scores   162
A3.4   Means and standard deviations for the long- and
       short-form total scores by managerial level   162

Acknowledgments

It's been a ten-year collaborative journey since J. Douglas Toma at Penn told me "Leadership in Balance" could be a book, and A. G. Lafley, Michael J. Graham, S. J., and Michael Conaton enabled access to elite groups of leaders who candidly shared their thinking and experiences. Bob McDonald and Ellen Mazza opened to us the rich wisdom of kanji; Dave Kucia and Sue Bensman created striking figures; and Pete Kucia and Kristin Kucia-Stauder seasoned me with challenging questions. Dave Hellkamp focused our attention on the deeper dimension of leaders. Bob Wubbolding, Marla Phillips, and Shari Mickey Boggs provided encouraging reviews; Phil Jones strengthened our metrics; and Judy and Dave Lococo, assisted by Arlene Coffaro, quarterbacked the final submission of our manuscript *Leadership in Balance: New Habits of the Mind*. John Kucia Jr. and Emily K. Bell offered regular family support, and Greg Rust caught us both on film. All the while, my dear Mary Cat was steadfast by my side. To all of you, I say thank you. We could not have accomplished this without each of you.

Linda would like to acknowledge the support and encouragement of her husband, Ron, throughout the long process of researching and coauthoring this book.

Both authors would like to acknowledge Dr. Mark Nagy, department head of Xavier University's Industrial and Organizational Psychology Department, Dr. Dalia Diab, professor in Xavier University's Industrial and Organizational Psychology Department, and Dr. Diab's class members for their excellent research assistance with the leadership assessment instruments used in the research and writing of this book. They are as follows: Ashley Brown, Chuck Cooper, Brandy Fitzpatrick, Christina Foster, Bryce Hansell, Amy Luthanen, Whitney Ohmer, Brittany Opdyke, Lisa Peterson, Nicole Sanders, Harrison Sibert, Jesse Simpson, and Chelsea Wymer.

Introduction

Leadership in Balance: New Habits of the Mind

In this book, we develop the premise that leaders are built from the inside out, hence the importance of their way of thinking.

Over the last several years, many excellent books have been published on the topic of leadership and the characteristics of successful leaders. Our purpose with this book is to join and enrich the conversation of these important works with a focus on addressing a deeper dimension for leaders. Many wise authors have come before us to establish a foundation for the deeper dive we have taken in exploring how leaders in balance actually think and then act on that thinking.

If you say, "I like the way that person thinks," it is more than a casual observation about a style or set of leadership characteristics and behaviors and more than a way of leading. You are making a critical judgment about a leader's way of seeing and understanding; a leader's way of thinking and interpreting meaning for their organization, which paves the way for the strategies, decisions, and actions of the leader and the future direction of the organization.

So where do we join this important conversation and how will we enrich it? Read on.

In *The Necessary Revolution*,[1] Peter Senge tackles the global leadership challenge of creating a sustainable world that can successfully address "three interconnected areas—energy and transportation, food and water material waste and toxicity, and the consequent imbalances that result when too many resources are concentrated in too few hands." Senge believes that globalization has brought a new level of interdependence between nations and regions of the world. He also believes that you can influence a natural living system, but not control it. In order to address this global leadership challenge, there is an urgent need for a revised way of thinking, with nature and not machines as our inspiration, and core capabilities such as seeing systems, collaboration across boundaries, and creating versus problem solving. He focuses his message not only on the traditional leaders of the hierarchy like the CEO and president, but also on people who don't think of themselves as leaders working deep within their organizations, perhaps operating as part of an untapped, talented, and creative informal network.

Leadership in Balance: New Habits of the Mind is a perfect companion book for the readers of *The Necessary Revolution*. We agree with Senge that it is time for a mental map that will address the challenge of leading change in the twenty-first century. Our current research results, drawn from seasoned leaders of a cross-section of organizations, confirm the value and validity of a portfolio of new professional development and coaching tools. "The Collaboration Equation," "The DNA of Collaboration: The Kucia Balance Framework,"[2] "Eight Ways of Thinking of a Leader in Balance," and a "Leadership in Balance" assessment instrument are all aids that complement, enrich, and deepen an understanding of this topic.

In *The Future of Management*,[3] Gary Hamel begins with the questions, "What does the future of management look like to you? How will tomorrow's successful companies be organized and managed?" Hamel observes that the practice of management is not evolving as fast as the business challenges presented by a more complex, global, and digitalized, web-connected environment. He states, "These new realities call for new organizational and managerial capabilities." Hamel refers to the "managerial DNA" of the traditional, industrial-military command-and-control style and describes the challenge of this essential area for change as the need to "reinvent your company's DNA." Throughout the book, Hamel suggests the need for different ways of seeing, understanding, and thinking about the value and talents of employees and the need for different approaches for organizing and leading. He suggests a twenty-first-century networked kind of organization as a way of spreading power and influence that harvests and connects this talent and generates creativity and innovation. This challenges the tradition of the hierarchy and the leaders who have been in control—hence, the rub.

Leadership in Balance offers valuable support and a solution to Hamel's rub as we develop the premise that the leadership required for a living organization in a global society calls for different habits of the mind; a fundamental shift from emphasis on leadership in control to leadership in balance and from a leader's way of behaving to a leader's ways of thinking. We offer a construct—*The Kucia Balance Framework*—that brings order and a deeper understanding of the complex and sometimes, paradoxical challenges of collaborative leadership and the capabilities and capacities required to succeed in our global society. These challenges are best met by a powerful model of a collaborative leader who can balance the best use of the hierarchy with the network to address the competing forces of continuity and change, and of competition and collaboration, as driven by the external forces of the market, guided by the internal values of mission and purpose. After laying this foundation, we dig deeper to identify the eight ways of thinking of a leader in balance, which replaces control with balance, approaches leadership as a relationship not a position, thinks outside of the pyramid, understands that at the center of collaboration is a personal comfort with valuing of diversity of people, ideas, and ways of thinking.

In Hamel's final chapter, he calls for today's leaders to "take every opportunity you can to get your associates thinking more deeply about their managerial DNA and how it may need to change." *Leadership in Balance* is the next book readers will find valuable as they work to develop the collaborative gene to strengthen their individual and organizational DNA.

In *Judgment: How Winning Leaders Make Great Calls*,[4] Noel Tichy and Warren Bennis develop the thesis that making good judgment calls is the essential job of a leader; that judgment is the core, the nucleus, of leadership; and that good judgment depends on how you think as much as what you know. They meticulously develop a framework for "demystifying the leadership judgment process." As a result of their thorough review of current literature, Tichy and Bennis conclude that not much is written about this area of leadership because it's hard.

Leadership in Balance offers a timely complement to *Judgment* and provides a broader context, and perhaps a more integrated image, for understanding the role of judgment, experience, and intuition in the performance of a leader. We focus on the importance of a leader's way of seeing and understanding, a leader's way of thinking and interpreting meaning to their organization, the foundation that paves the way for the strategies, decisions, and actions of the leader and the future direction of the organization.

Tichy and Bennis end their book with the statement, "Judgment is the essential genome of leadership," suggesting there is something more foundational than practices and behaviors, something inside to be developed in the nature of a leader. *Leadership in Balance: New Habits of the Mind* will be an ideal companion book for those who want to read more about a hard, deeper, and essential dimension of the study of leadership.

In *Wikinomics: How Mass Collaboration Changes Everything*,[5] Don Tapscott and Anthony Williams describe an important business paradigm shift that challenges the conventional wisdom and traditional command-and-control functioning of the hierarchy. This network-oriented business model is based upon the competitive principles of openness, peering, sharing, and acting globally. It "opens its doors to the world" and coinnovates and shares resources, once closely guarded, in order to harness the power of mass collaboration.

We believe there is much to be learned about the role of collaboration in leading change in a living organization, and there is great value derived from the emerging role of networks as purpose-driven structures critical to the process of collaboration and change. However, instead of replacing the hierarchy, we believe networks can be skillfully used to augment the hierarchy in a balanced manner to encourage a diversity of thought, innovation, and creativity to spread influence and power, and to organize learning communities of disciplined people, thought, and action inside an organization that connect with networks outside.

Tapscott and Williams suggest that, today, successful leaders must think differently about how to compete and be profitable and embrace the art and science of collaboration they call "Wikinomics." To that end, they key on "the ability to integrate the talents of dispersed individuals and organizations" as "*the* defining competency for managers and firms." In their final chapter titled "Collaborative Minds: The Power of Thinking Differently,"[6] the authors ask questions such as "What kind of leaders will be required to bring about this new corporate world?" and "How do we rewire our brain to think differently…and develop a collaborative mind?" *Wikinomics* ends with a call for leaders to prepare "their collaborative minds because companies will need unique leadership capabilities to work in collaborative environments."

With a shift in thinking from control to balance and from ways of behaving to ways of thinking, our self-assessment instruments capture a leader's balance across eight ways of thinking related to strategy (head), culture (heart), and leadership (hand). The assessments were administered to successful leaders in resilient organizations to test their efficacy in today's complex global society.

In *Presence: An Exploration of Profound Change in People, Organizations and Society,*[7] Senge et al. believe "the deeper dimensions of transformational change are a largely unexplored territory in current management and leadership, and the blind spot concerns not what leaders do and how they do it, but who we are and the inner place or source from which we operate, both individually and collectively."

We agree fully. In this book, we plumb those depths to understand the ways of thinking, seeing, understanding, and being that give rise to the response/behavior of a leader in balance. Senge et al. believe, "You can influence a natural living system, but not control it." We envision an organization as a living being, much like Arie de Geus in *The Living Company*.[8] Consequently, we suggest it is time for an approach that addresses the challenge of leading change in the twenty-first century.

In *Resonant Leadership*,[9] Richard Boyatzis and Annie McKee built upon the Emotional Intelligence (EI) work of Daniel Coleman and their own primal leadership to spread the message that great leaders are resonant within themselves and attuned to others. Similarly, *Leadership in Balance* develops the theme that a leader and an organization are built from the inside out. Boyatzis and McKee demonstrate methods for cultivating mindfulness, hope, and compassion in one's self and others, while we enrich and deepen the conversation by offering a leader's way of seeing, of understanding, and of thinking and being that give rise to the behaviors of a leader in balance. We apply this to answer the question "leadership to what end—short-term gain or long-term survival?" Boyatsiz and McKee suggest a pie chart (body, mind, heart, and spirit) as an instrument for self-valuation of a leader's balance in life that divides into sharp wedges the parts of a whole person with no sense of integration. "The DNA of Collaboration: The Kucia Balance Framework" develops the powerful image of an integrated person, a collaborative leader of a living organization, and provides a construct for understanding the complex and sometimes, paradoxical challenges leaders face.

In *The World Is Flat*,[10] Thomas Friedman builds upon his 1999 book, *The Lexus and the Olive Tree: Understanding Globalization*,[11] in which he opened to us a way of thinking about and understanding what seemed to be the uncontrollable chaos of globalization. In *The World Is Flat*,[12] Friedman shares with us ten major forces (e.g., workflow software, outsourcing, offshoring, supply chaining, and the steroids) that have started to converge and work together in ways that have created a flatter, global playing field. We welcome Friedman's insights because he supports and adds expert testimony to our premise that it is time for a paradigm for leadership in this global society in which the world has begun to move from a primarily vertical (command and control) value creation model to an increasingly horizontal (connect and collaborate) model.

Leadership in Balance defines and develops the competencies of a deeper dimension of a leader who truly believes that the challenges of change no longer are adequately addressed by leadership in control, but by leadership in balance. Friedman states, "The best companies are the best collaborators and, that in the flat world, more and more business will be done through collaborations within and between companies." He believes things are becoming so complex that no single firm or department is going to be able to master them alone. This book provides a framework to support Friedman's belief.

In *Executive Intelligence*,[13] Justin Menkes, the author, focuses on describing and assessing characteristics that ensure leadership success in today's complex world of work, which is also the focus of this book. He frames these characteristics as skills that flow from one's IQ level and minimizes the importance of EI. *Leadership in Balance* elevates EI to a higher order of importance in predicting leadership success.

As you can see from a review of the literature, readers of *Leadership in Balance: New Habits of the Mind* will gain a deeper understanding of the art, practice, and discipline of purpose-driven collaboration and will learn how new leadership habits of the mind will positively impact an organization's learning, growth, and change. Finally, readers will embrace a new appreciation for the value of nurturing "the gene of collaboration" in the DNA of all leaders throughout their long-living organizations in this twenty-first-century global society.

Part I

Building the Fundamentals

Chapter 1

Leader as Brand

"Brands must deliver solutions not just benefits. They must be more than trademarks; they must be trustmarks." These thoughts about the power of branding were expressed by A. G. Lafley, chairman and chief executive officer of Procter & Gamble (P&G), to Michael J. Graham, S. J., president of Xavier University, and a room full of Xavier vice presidents, deans, and directors during a strategy-planning session the Xavier leadership was conducting. Lafley knew that the message he was about to deliver concerning the power of a brand and the importance of trust must be heard and embraced deep into an organization. Lafley freely shared his expertise and the renowned marketing knowledge of P&G as the first of important emerging themes began to surface. He keyed in on certain realities about branding: it impacts the way others think about us; it provides an empowering way to align actions, behaviors, and choices; and inspirationally, it reflects who we are today and who we want to be in the future. Branding brings to life our unique combination of attributes for the people who find them important and compelling.

By the end of the day, the group of Xavier leaders had gained a new way of understanding the meaning and expectations created by a brand. It became clear that a brand is more than a stamp on the surface of an organization or its products or services. In short, *a brand is a promise*. It is essential that the brand promise is clearly understood by the people inside the organization because a brand is built from the inside out.

A few weeks later, President Graham was intrigued to receive a handwritten letter from Lafley in which he shared some observations linking strategy to execution. To Graham's surprise, Lafley wrote that both of them are "brands" of their respective institutions. Although Lafley and Graham head very different businesses, the challenge for leading change in their respective institutions is very much alike. Both Lafley and Graham share a way of seeing—understanding their organizations as living entities—communities of talented people, rather than machines to make money; both institutions depend heavily on knowledge workers to accomplish their purpose; both are challenged to lead with a vision that will grow the business through the work of an organization of talented people with the ability to learn and build community. Both must fully engage the commitment, talents, creativity, and leadership capabilities of the organization in order to accomplish the purpose of an institution so it will continue to serve society far into the future.

The suggestion that a leader is a *brand* was too provocative for Graham to let go without more dialogue. Lafley and Graham asked Kucia to set up a lunch meeting with them where they could discuss the topics of *brand* and *trust*. Graham wanted to explore more about the assertion that the leader is a brand, that is, the person who embodies the institutional brand promise. Lafley wanted to consider with Graham a corollary challenge—low public trust in institutions and their leaders today. The meeting was scheduled and Kucia was present to listen and learn.

Since Graham wanted to learn, he listened as Lafley, a master leader who teaches, began to share his thoughts on a subject he knows well. Lafley began, "Like it or not, we are public figures and you and I don't have any choice in that matter. Everybody that has any kind of interest in the university, in your case, or in the corporation, in mine—those stakeholders cannot separate us from the brand. It will be impossible for you. Even if you tell them you want to separate the two—they won't be able to separate the two." Graham expressed to Lafley that raising his awareness to this fundamental reality opened him to a new way of thinking about his role as a leader.

Lafley went on to explain his thinking to Graham about brand by sharing the story of the basic strategy he employed as he began his responsibilities in 2000 during a difficult time for the company. "I mean to make it real simple. I worked with customers who are our retail customers; I worked with analysts and investors; and I worked with employees. The primary objective with employees was hope and confidence. With the investors, it was trust. With retail customers it was, 'we want to be your best supplier, offering the best brands, the best innovations, the best service, the best everything.'" Lafley described how he traveled around the world and saw every one of them face-to-face, one-on-one, with no entourage. "I wasn't selling anything; I was listening, and I let them take their shots." He was demonstrating to his stakeholders that they were important; that he was accessible and wanted to hear from them firsthand. That is when it became clear to Lafley that he was becoming the brand—"the promise of something to someone." Lafley then explained how he was trying to elevate all the other "carriers or owners of the brand." Now when he talks to employees, he tells them, "Like it or not, *we* are the brand."

Lafley and Graham agreed that there are lots of risks, but that's the way it is. "It is just their [the stakeholder's] expectation; it's not anything that you choose." Graham observed that he is the current face of the university as he explained, "Although the person's relationship is really with the university, you embody that in a way that is surprising." Continuing to explore the challenge of addressing stakeholder expectations, Graham admitted to Lafley, "I know the promise that we make to our students. What I don't understand is the kind of promise that the university makes externally in some unspoken way." Graham was referring to various groups of people, stakeholders who believe the university should be making some kind of promise. He is held accountable for whatever the promise might be, whether it's the church's actions or inactions, the university and its position within the constellation of institutions of higher education in the area, or the university's relationships with local neighborhoods. "What are those promises—the images or ideas in folks' heads that are somehow focused on you? You're never quite sure what the performance standards are, except that you're not meeting them—like your stockholders." Hence, in the minds of stakeholders, Graham is held responsible for fulfilling promises and meeting expectations, known and unknown.

In response to Graham, Lafley shared what he has learned. "If you don't clarify the promise, or be clear that there isn't a promise, they [stakeholders] are assuming that there is one." The reality he discovered is that all stakeholders are assuming you are going to deliver something to them and for them. Lafley continued, "Unless you're clear about what the relationship is going to be, whether there is going to be a promise and what the promise is going to be, you're left in this situation where you don't know what they've assumed at best and, at worst, they're really disappointed in you and your institution because you're not delivering, and half the time you don't even know against what; for what?" That was the part Lafley said was "mind boggling."

Lafley explained how he tries to be "very transparent about what the purpose is, what the goals are, and what the strategies are, so everybody understands that if we accomplish them, everybody will benefit. So it's sort of, all for one, one for all." Lafley's strategy is to stay with one very short, relatively simple agenda that he repeats over and over again. The first few times his listeners say, "Okay, I hear you." A few more repetitions later they say, "I think I understand you." A few more yet and they say, "Maybe I'll trust you; maybe I won't." Finally, they say, "Okay, we've got a deal." With this, Lafley emphasizes the intentional process he employs to gain trust and buy-in to purpose, goals, and strategies, and the stages a stakeholder must move through—I hear, I understand, I trust—before a stakeholder's commitment is secured.

Lafley and Graham agreed that this current time "is the most collaborative they have ever seen their organization." This observation reflects a significant leadership and cultural change that both organizations have experienced over the years, recalling a time when "the bully boys were in power at P&G" and the president ran Xavier "like a south-side Chicago monsignor ran his parish," observations made by longtime insiders from P&G and Xavier.

But Lafley and Graham realize they have tough acts to follow, both from the success of their predecessors and their own successful track records since assuming their leadership positions. They realize that growing the business may not only mean getting larger and increasing revenues, but it also means changing the way they work and evolving the business as influenced by the market realities of globalization. Ultimately, they think about their legacy: "How do I leave the company because of the choices I have made?"

As the conversation continued, Lafley turned their attention to the importance of organizational capabilities and competencies—as if they were "stones or bricks in the wall," the solid foundation for an organization. The answer for "how to win is all about capabilities and competencies." P&G leadership has identified the skills and capabilities they must have as an organization to be the best in the world at what they do. Lafley explained, "We make somebody who's at the top of the organization responsible for developing the capabilities and then we try to measure. We try to measure how we're doing. How good is our capability, really, versus the best that's out there?" Lafley and Graham began to explore the questions, "What is the combination of capabilities that is Xavier and P&G, but not just isolated capabilities? They have to connect, network with each other . . . all stitched together." Lafley continued to develop the meaning of connecting and began to integrate the concepts of this conversation to stitch them together. "I really think the difference in our world is brands, people, our capabilities and systems, and our culture because our culture comes out of what you do; it comes out of how you do what you do. Your culture is the character of the company. I don't think the purpose, the character, the values, the principles ever change; they are sort of no compromise. Everything else changes because you need and we need different capabilities in 2008 than we did in 1977."

Graham acknowledged, "What we've got to do is get much better at taking joint collective responsibility for the enterprise, but universities are highly-balkanized kinds of realities." To this assertion, Lafley responded, "If you choose to create horizontal capabilities and strengths, you involve the entire community and organization, and then you encourage mutual collaboration, because the truth of the matter is you can't achieve the competency or capability unless you get some level of collaboration." That requires a very high level of integration that is more difficult to run because it's not as clear. Who is the boss; who is in charge; who is responsible for the outcome? Lafley's responded, "The answer is it depends on what we're doing. The boss might be the boss in one situation; but might be support in another situation; might not even be involved in a third situation." Both Graham and Lafley agreed that this could be accomplished in a university and a company with bright people who are well educated and who have "reasonable EQs to go with their IQs. If you can collaborate, it's a big advantage because most organizations have difficulty doing it." Lafley added, "The other advantage of this sort of integration is that it reinforces organizational culture and enables you to use your culture to drive collaboration. You can use it to drive capabilities that stretch across functions. So it sort of all fits." When this kind of collaborative culture permeates the entire organization and is shared by faculty, staff, and administrators, then "the brand promise has been tried and found not to be wanting at that moment. It's one of those moments of truth. This is a sign that there is alignment of the brand, the people, and our promise to stakeholders."

Graham shared with Lafley that in moving away from a hierarchical, top-down approach, leading an organization "empowers a broader cross-section of people to embody the brand and, ultimately, that's real reality. But, does that slow you down; make you less nimble now; less able to turn on a dime than you were before?" Lafley's response was surprising and somewhat counterintuitive. Instead of taking more time to involve more people, Lafley said, "I think we're faster; I think we're more responsive because people understand that the consumer is the boss. They'll respond to the customer; they'll respond to the competitor; and they'll respond to the marketplace." He continued by explaining that P&G has high levels of decentralization because they believe that the people closest to the consumer and the marketplace have a much better feel for what's going on, so they should make the decision. "When there's something urgent, an emergency or a threat, they are actually pretty quick." He continued, "but we are deliberate and slow when we're trying to get everybody to work on creating one capability that we want to have across the whole organization. It takes a while to put capability building blocks in place."

Lafley observed, "At P&G we talk a lot about failure, too. Failure is great. Failure is not failure; failure is learning. But, good learning is when you fail cheap and you fail fast. Bad learning is when we've lost millions of dollars and then we finally figure it out." Failure is learning, learning is growth, and growth is change. Consequently, a leader who thinks of failure as an opportunity for learning creates a healthy environment for collaboration, innovation, and creativity.

Lafley and Graham agreed that attention to detail is really important to both a university and a corporation. For both organizations, it ultimately comes down to many small things done very well, "delivering on the promise with a kind of relentlessness of purpose imbedded in people throughout the organization."

Both agreed that they can't do it alone. The leadership of their organizations is judged daily by employees' observations of the leader's behavior and by consumers' observations of the behavior of the employees. Lafley observed, "People don't do what you say; they do what you do; they watch. You can talk until you're blue in the face, but they're going to do what you do." They both concluded that if the leader takes care of delivering on the promise and achieving the mission of providing a needed service to society, the profit would take care of itself.

Following the emerging themes thus far, this began to open my eyes to a new way of seeing, understanding, and thinking about both leader and brand. I began to understand that a brand is a promise and that a brand is built from the inside out. Developing the premise that a leader is a brand and that a leader and their organization are built from the inside out suggests a new conversation that is broader than a style of leadership, more than a set of leadership characteristics and behaviors, and deeper than a way of leading. Instead, in this book we are probing something that is deeper and more robust. We are exploring the way of seeing and understanding and the way of thinking and being that is inside the foundation of a leader who embodies the brand, its values and its promise, one who sets the tone and interprets meaning for the organization.

Although they could have continued on the topic of brand, time was running out, and so they turned their attention to the topic of trust. Lafley listened as Graham, a master teacher who leads, skillfully guided them through a shared reflection on the issue of declining trust in leaders and institutions. They both realize that trust is the foundation for their success as leaders and the success of their respective institutions. Lafley framed the issue he wanted to explore as follows: "Most of the brands we sell are sold on the basis of trust." He observed that this is one of the lowest periods of trust in American history since 1900 and that "CEO is a four-letter word now—people who do my job—and, frankly, government officials, politicians—just about anybody in authority—are not trusted. So, when you're entrusted with an institution like Xavier and P&G that runs on trust," Lafley asked Graham, "what can we do to rebuild trust?"

Graham began by saying, "Act trustworthy." He agreed that right now we have a historically low moment of public morale and trust, but that there's also a "great desire for looking around and finding places in which one can repose one's trust." He observed that the bitterness and disillusionment he sees is that "there are so few places and even the traditionally reputable ones have been found to have clay feet. I'm a priest. Well, this is a great line of work to be in these days! If there is a lack of trust in the leader and the leader is the brand that challenges the trust in the institution."

Graham suggested that there are lots of people out there who are "looking at you with hope in their eyes and doubt in the back of their mind." Graham said he approaches the contemporary climate in the way he has always approached being a professor on campus. "One attempts to be someone who seems to be living a life that he likes, that seems to him to be worth living. I think it comes back to executing fundamentals well. So how is it that I should be behaving as a priest? What is it that people look to me specifically to do and to be? How can I not simply preach that message, but embody it in some way and, therefore, how does the institution itself, as a university, do that as well?" Graham shared that before he became president of Xavier, a trustee said to him something that he will never forget: "In a very large measure, I need to remember to take care of my own soul because the soul of the institution begins in mine." Graham noted that the trustee's words "really helped me shape, fundamentally, how I think about what it is that I do as president." Here, Graham is suggesting that the way he thinks sets the foundation and, in a sense, paves the way for his strategies and behaviors that follow.

For Graham, attention to certain things as priest and professor are evident and important because it helps remind him why it is that he is doing this in the first place. "There are a lot of people out there who could do a better job of running a university as a technical enterprise with these systems and opportunities and all this kind of stuff—folks who come up from within university administration who've done the comprehensive university thing and are expert with respect to marketing or budgeting, or whatever it is. But I bring a certain perspective that cannot be otherwise brought to the university except through the pastoral side of my own vocation. So, to stay in contact with that is to stay in contact with the thing that makes it possible for me to have a voice in an industry that's a distinctive one, and to bring a distinctive edge to a particular place." Graham believes that there is more to being a president than mastering the technical competencies of the business of running a university. The "more" relates to the way of thinking and being, the way of understanding a situation and interpreting its meaning to an organization.

Graham described the challenge of trying to figure out when to "have the right set of glasses on as one is reading these reports, or dealing with this personnel issue, or whatever kind of routine matter that crosses the desk of any president in any university in the country." But, somehow, "it's supposed to look different, feel different to me because of who I am. That's a work in progress."

For Graham, the trust issue is both a crisis and an opportunity that may not be addressed in traditional terms. "Trust is always earned. I think what one does is inspire people to trust by tapping into their hopes and dreams and figuring out how to engage them in the enterprise. I think that our stock in trade is to establish trust." Ultimately, Graham felt that hope is key. "I suspect people do have this sense that wouldn't it be better to live in a world where one could trust people? The more I think about this, the more I think if trust is given freely, then it's easier for trust to be earned. In other words, I think, in adult-to-adult situations, one party has to move—one party has to say, 'Okay, I'm going to trust you,' and then trust gets built. So it's not one-way—it's mutual."

Graham and Lafley concluded that the way trust happens is to say, "Well, alright, what do you need? What can I do for you? What hope do you have; what vision do you have? How would you like things to be better than they are? How can I help that happen in some way that's appropriate to me and the job that I have?" In short, they must listen, learn, and deliver on the promise.

The emerging themes that have surfaced throughout this dialogue on brand and trust begin to suggest the importance of new ways of thinking and understanding, new habits of the mind, and true learning that form the foundation for a leader's response and behavior that follows. The way a leader sees and understands him/herself and the world around them and their place within it are the deeper dimensions of leadership. We believe it is critical, if not urgent, to explore these deeper dimensions, now, for the benefit of leaders of long-living organizations who are charged with addressing the challenges of leadership and change in this twenty-first-century global society. In pursuit of that end, the chapters of our book are organized with a goal of opening us all to raised awareness and a new realization that the challenge of leading change is not about leadership in control, instead it is about leadership in balance—a deeper dimension.[1]

Chapter 2

A New Model of Leadership for a Living Organization

What can a university leader and a corporate leader learn from one another about leading change in their respective organizations? What difference would it make for a leader to think of an organization as a community of talented people rather than a machine to make money and how differently would that person lead his/her organization? What is the influence inside an organization whose leader is fondly nicknamed, "Neutron Jack" (Jack Welsh of GE) or the "Prince of Darkness" (Ed Artz of P&G)? All of this leads us to ask the next strategic questions: Leadership for what purpose? Who is that person? What kind of leader must he/she be? Who is capable of leading a long-living organization in this century's global society? In *The Living Company*, Arie de Geus gives us a start by defining a long-living organization as an entity that has survived for 100 years or more because it has developed the ability to learn as an organization and improve, to build community, to construct relationships with entities within and outside of itself, and to govern its own growth and evolution effectively.[1]

To answer these questions, we interviewed an impressive group of practitioners of leadership who shared their thoughts freely. The most real, honest, and natural way to collect their thoughts was to let the leaders take the lead and allow them to tell their story. Some were corporate executives and trustees;

others were university executives and trustees. Some were considered scholars in their fields; others were scholars of leadership. All were practitioners of leadership in either for-profit or not-for-profit institutions that were created to serve society in some special manner. From the observations they offered, a composite image of a collaborative leader emerged.

Authentic collaborative leadership is not a technique. The collaborative leader, first, is a person who approaches leadership as a relationship rather than a position, one who shows respect for people by listening closely to them and by creating bonds of friendship and a sense of camaraderie in the organization. To that end, the collaborative leader engenders a sense of personal humility balanced with enormous organizational ego, thus placing the needs of the organization over those of themselves. This leader models such behavior in order to create loyalty to the institution rather than to one's self to build organizational capability. This leader is very comfortable with the notion of collaboration, is open to learning, and sees value in collaboration as a means of achieving leadership and organizational ends. This leader understands that collaboration is cultural, but it's more a business necessity than cultural. The collaborative leader is a pragmatist who believes that you can't get good business results if you can't collaborate. However, there is no inherent benefit for collaborating if it's not going to produce a desired business result. Results are the reason to collaborate.

The collaborative leader understands that there are two purposes and, therefore, two benefits of collaboration—the creation of the idea and the execution of the idea. Collaboration is a means to an end—to reach better decisions and implement them better, to get the right answer and get it executed. Successful execution is a challenging part of collaboration. A danger of collaboration is that it can become a morass of endless conversation or a homogenizing process that looks like an effort at consensus building and, therefore, often doesn't get anything accomplished. The reasons for collaboration are to accomplish something; to solve a problem; to get something done.

This leader espouses and demonstrates a positive regard for collaboration because of productive, successful experiences that have resulted in better strategies, better decisions, and better execution, complemented by a certain amount of personal maturity and new insights. The collaborative leader understands that in today's complex environment of constant change and increasing global competition, the overwhelming job of leadership is more than one person can accomplish alone. The leader needs help, is able to openly admit mistakes, and realizes that a competitive advantage can be gained through harnessing the power of interdependence and purpose-driven collaboration as a way of proceeding as a leader and as an organization. The operative word is leadership, not collaboration.

This person realizes that the leader sets the tone for the organization by what is said and, more importantly, by what is done and what is valued. This leader models the behavior expected of others and establishes the moral and ethical values of the organization by addressing issues with honesty, trust, integrity, respect, and affection for the dignity of others. This leader brings social and emotional intelligence to leadership. The leader's transparent manner, way of making decisions, and personal behavior nurtures trust and communicates a set of expectations and preferences for the behavior of other leaders within the organization.

Lafley said, "If there is resistance to change, the collaborative leader understands that one must meet resistance; don't hold back. Go in to get a better bead on what's happening. The collaboration that is required at this moment is a collaboration of desires to steel the collective nerve. To that end, the leader realizes that trust is an essential foundation for collaboration and must be balanced with the normal instincts for competition."

Collaboration begins at the top, among the senior administrators who must demonstrate their own ability to trust and to collaborate among themselves. This leader knows that collaboration not only occurs at the top of an organization, but also must happen as A. G. Lafley said, "In the bowels of a truly collaborative organization." Thus, this leader embodies the "brand promise" for the organization, which is both a noble and humbling role to perform. The many stakeholders, both inside and outside the organization, derive an important aspect of their relationship with the institution through their real or perceived image of the leader.

The collaborative leader balances the present reality with movement toward the future reality and ponders, "What is the shape of the company for the future? What is the structure?" This leader focuses attention on the purpose, mission, and values of the institution as a way of raising people's motivation to levels above personal interest, emphasizing the success of the institution as a whole through service to society in some special way. This leader understands the challenge of balancing continuity with change. Sole focus on profits and the bottom line may lead to short-term thinking and decisions that do not give adequate consideration to the long-term life of the organization.

Creating a culture of collaboration inside the organization, balanced with competition focused outside the organization is critical, so that we can energetically collaborate inside and compete outside. The collaborative leader truly believes that what drives the numbers for corporations and universities is the mission. If we accomplish our mission, the numbers take care of themselves. It turns out we make a lot of money. Interdependence and collaboration are essential means to accomplishing the purpose and mission of any organization.

For collaboration to work in any organization there are certain capabilities and competencies that individuals and the organization must acquire; there is a realization that the leader must first be comfortable with these. At the very center of collaboration are openness and a valuing of diversity of people, ideas, and ways of thinking requiring a level of individual and organizational cultural competence. The leader accomplishes this by allowing people to learn, grow, and trust one another by spending time listening and getting to know each other in a kind of ad hoc collaborative community—a powerful concept, a network of collaborative leadership.

Collaboration requires an organization and its leaders to learn, grow, and improve, and thus adapt and change. The collaborative leader believes teaching and leadership have a great deal in common and personally relates to being both a teacher and a leader. The art of teaching is to help people come to a new understanding of their reality and themselves. "I can be successful and convince people to change because it is in their best interest."

Leading by teaching is an important part of the collaborative leader's responsibility that can be accomplished by asking hard questions and stimulating learning, all in search of reality and truth. This leads to setting the right course and creating the right strategy for the organization in a disciplined, deliberate, and intentional manner. But the leader knows that to be a good teacher you must be a good learner, which requires a leader to listen, to be observant, and to be curious. It requires the leader to admit to not having all the answers, thus being vulnerable and open to learning. The leader encourages learning through coaching, teaching, stimulating learning models, and placing value on learning for the organization and individuals. The collaborative leader values learning in the real world rather than intellectualizing and seeks in-person contact at the touch points where conflicts arise. But after due reflection, the collaborative leader knows when it's time to make a decision and take action otherwise it frustrates everyone. It does no good to know something if we don't translate it into action to improve something. The leader makes certain to always close the loop with a purpose.

Basic to collaboration is a willingness to share power and spread leadership, authority, and responsibility to all levels throughout the organization. The leader must be comfortable championing the development of leadership and collaboration skills and capabilities throughout the organization. This is accomplished by changing organizational structures and is

balanced through use of the network to augment the hierarchy. Use of the network is particularly valuable when a challenge is complex, requiring a diversity of disciplined thinking,
creativity, and innovation across boundaries inside and outside
the organization. This kind of collaborative work community
or learning network changes relationships, changes behaviors,
and changes the culture of an organization. It results in new
competencies and capabilities, including disciplined people,
disciplined thinking, and disciplined actions, thus creating a
network of influence, power, and learning to augment the hierarchy throughout an organization.

The collaborative leader ultimately envisions a new structure
for the organization and an internal network of creative people
connecting with an external global network—all collaborating
and working on issues that require more learning, entrepreneurial, creative, and innovative actions. The leader realizes that
knowing how and when to unify as well as orchestrate these
very different organizational structures—the hierarchy and the
network calls for skills and judgment that are oftentimes based
more on intuition and instinct than data. Frankly, much of leadership is far more intuitive than planned. You never know from
moment to moment how things will play out. But it has to be
fluid—fluid in the situation, fluid in the decision being made.

Cultural competence and a comfort with a diversity of ideas
and identities, such as genders and ethnicities, are essential for
the leader of an organization with a collaborative culture. A
leader believes that diversity of gender, race, nationality, and
ethnicity is an enormously strengthening factor. Involving
other people and getting the right balance is the challenge.
The leader believes that when people are collaborating well
there is a degree of comfort and trust and more potential for
people to learn. The leader strongly believes that collaboration,
cooperation, and interdependence are a business and a cultural
necessity.

Collaboration involves sharing power and spreading control
allowing for a diversity of ideas. Collaboration calls for changing

structures and relationships that at times may alter the sense of privilege often signaled by the traditional hierarchy. The collaborative leader knows that collaboration is hard work, perhaps harder than command and control, and is certainly not the slow, soft side of management. Instead, collaboration requires a business purpose, courage, and commitment. Sometimes conflict is required as disagreement helps to differentiate the nature of a problem or how its solution can be expected.[2]

A Reflection

We know from our experience that leaders and their organizations transform incrementally—they learn, they grow, and they change. As leaders become the person they are meant to be, so do their organizations. As we begin to answer strategic questions about leadership, we offer an image of an integrated, collaborative leader of a living organization that blends the characteristics of de Geus's long-living company with the characteristics of a collaborative leader—elements of both individual and organizational capabilities and competencies as:

- a person who thinks critically and reflectively with the *head of a strategist*, able to lead an organization that has the ability to learn (sensitive to the environment) and govern its own growth and evolution (wise financing and use of resources);
- a person who makes choices and decisions with a *moral and ethical heart*, able to lead an organization that has the ability to build community and a persona for itself (cohesion and identity); and
- a person who executes strategy with the *hand of a collaborative leader*, able to lead an organization that has the ability to build constructive relationships with other entities within and outside (tolerance and decentralization).[3]

Chapter 3

It's Time for a Different Leadership Paradigm

We believe it is time for a new leadership paradigm to support how an organization survives and thrives in a global society. A "paradigm" is simply a mental map about how to navigate in the world around us. Just like any map, mental maps can be wrong; they can be outdated. Navigating the global society of the twenty-first century will require updated mental maps for the leaders of tomorrow.

In this chapter, we will explore how the following eight ways of thinking relate to the eight core competencies we believe are required to be a leader in balance:

- Approaches leadership as a relationship not a position
- Understands that the leader embodies the brand promise
- Is motivated by a higher purpose and believes that mission drives the numbers
- Understands collaboration must have a business purpose
- Thinks outside the pyramid in order to share power and spread leadership, authority, and responsibility
- Believes teaching and leadership have a great deal in common
- Understands that a personal comfort with and valuing of diversity are at the center of collaboration
- Believes that the challenge of leading change is not about leadership in control, but leadership in balance

Additionally, we'll delve into the positive impact these leadership competencies have on a wide range of organizations.

The first strength that we believe is essential for top leaders is *critical analysis.* We can break this competency into two parts: thinking and analysis. Thinking involves manipulation of sensations individuals pick up from the outside world through the eyes, ears, nose, tongue, and skin. These sensations are transmitted by the nerves to the brain which then translates, decodes, and encodes messages before sending them on throughout the nervous system. Analysis occurs when perceptions are turned into reactions based on concepts, ideas, assumptions, suppositions, inferences, hypotheses, and beliefs. Of course, our unique, individual worldview serves as a filter for all of these sensations and can get in the way of objective analysis.

A major component of critical analysis in the workplace is knowledge management, which can be described as knowing how to apply information and concepts to the *true* problem. Critical thinking involves knowing what information is important to the organization and what is superfluous. We've observed that critical analysis requires focus in the face of information overload. A critical thinker can select and use the appropriate technology to process information. Even if incoming data does not affect a critical thinker's immediate problem or issue, they discern who within the organization should have the data. Lastly, a critical thinker uses concepts and ideas they encounter to improve existing organizational processes by continually asking questions, such as, "Where in our organization can this idea be applied to improve results?"

Critical analysis certainly does not have to be cold, emotionless, or dispassionate. Actually, it can be very liberating to be free of past assumptions and the self-doubt that can result in making poor choices. Critical thinkers must keep lines of communication open to colleagues at all levels to keep valuable information flowing, which results in sound decisions.

Tom Cody at Macy's gave us a perfect example of how a false assumption can sneak into a seemingly logical, objective decision. He shared a story about how his organization used to provide free coffee on every floor of their corporate headquarters. When he and his finance department took a look at the money going out the door each month for coffee and supplies, like sugar for four hundred people, Tom concluded that, in lean times, the only thing to do was take out the coffee machines—and so he did. The assumption that he made was that this decision wouldn't matter to most people. It did. "One of my staff," he told us, "is still mad at me after nineteen years—and she doesn't even drink coffee!"

Critical analysis affects other leadership behaviors, of course, such as embracing diversity. A critical thinker is sensitive to stereotypes about people and waits to form an opinion about another's value to the organization until there is substantive information on which to base that opinion.

A critical thinker attempts to understand others' perspectives and reasons for engaging in particular behaviors in order to communicate effectively with them, taking them as they are as opposed to where he or she thinks they should be at any point. A critical thinker works well in a global environment because of a tolerance for ambiguity or ability to accept multiple interpretations of the same situation. Finally, critical thinkers are often curious about other people and the world around them, always seeking to understand how systems and processes work and how people work best within those systems and processes.

A leader who is not in balance might engage in critical analysis in a totally negative way, for example, searching for ways to tear down ideas without replacing them with viable options. When this happens, leaders cannot make a decision or make commitments to people, ideas, or plans. They fall back on tried and true approaches such as unilateral decision making. Leaders who operate constantly in the command-and-control posture fall into this category. Leaders who are not in balance tend to accept justifications for decisions and behaviors (of themselves and others) at face value without taking time to obtain sufficient facts or engage in intentional reflection, learning, and growth.

A second critical competency for the leader in balance is *reflection*. Reflection is looking back at events that have already occurred. Intentional reflection is setting time aside to positively and thoughtfully look back even when that reflection is not flattering. Intentional reflection is reviewing the past in order to make better decisions in the future.

We suggest using reflection to look forward as well as backward. Whenever a crisis occurs, leaders are forced to decide the best course of action and act quickly (and sometimes unilaterally). We believe that a leader in balance will pause before acting to draw on both instinct and experience to respond appropriately. Dr. Peter Chung, chairman of the Eminata Group, an education-based company headquartered in Vancouver, British Columbia, said in a 2008 article, "You have to search your soul and discover why you want to go in that direction." After a crisis has passed, contemplative leaders reflect on important lessons they've learned during the difficult time. They consider changes their organization can make to minimize the chance of reoccurrence of the same or similar crisis. Problems are viewed as learning opportunities for people throughout the organization.

One of the leaders we interviewed for this book provided an excellent example of a person who is intentionally reflective and self-aware. Bob McDonald, former CEO of Procter & Gamble said,

> I think the best leaders are highly self-aware and that, to me, is kind of like a common denominator. Those leaders who struggle lack self-awareness. Being reflective on one's self is all about character. Being reflective is not weak; it's strong. You have to be much more deliberate as a leader, much more thoughtful, and much more reflective to get the most out of those personal interactions that you have with others.

Don Washkewicz, chairman, CEO, and president of Parker Hannifin Corporation, was also strong in his views about intentional reflection. He said about reflecting on strategizing in his early days as new CEO,

> I felt it incumbent upon myself to figure out the strategy. I said that's what they're paying me for. I need to figure out where I want this company to go, and I need to put that, then, in terms where people can understand it.

Marilyn Shazor, former CEO of Southern Ohio Regional Transit Authority (SORTA), told us, "I often reflect on what I am not doing, what I can change personally that can make things better. I constantly work on this."

John Pepper, former CEO of Procter & Gamble, shared in his interview,

> You know, I'm conscious that what I do as a leader is seen by other people. I mean, I'm not blind to that, and I know that matters. I think of what I should be doing to be of service. If there's one thing I try to think about orienting toward, that's it.

A third critical competency for a leader in balance is *strategic perspective*. This perspective includes shareholders, consumers, the community, and employees. Jack Kraeutler, CEO of Meridian Bioscience, Inc., explains strategic perspective, "I am an observer and a listener. I do what makes sense to the consumer."

In her research with Robin Throckmorton on generational differences in the workplace for a recent book, *Bridging the Generation Gap*,[1] Linda Gravett interviewed five hundred people in each of the two youngest workplace generations, Generation X (Gen X) and Generation Y (Gen Y). She found that a compelling factor in enticing these employees to stay with an organization is trust, that is, they want to work in a high-trust work environment. A leader who can foster a high-trust work environment encourages people at all organizational levels to share ideas and suggestions to improve processes. She insists that information be shared, from something as straightforward as a new employee coming on board, to more complicated and sensitive information, such as errors in judgment on an annual report. A leader who fosters high trust is not stingy with praise and recognition; he acknowledges others who have helped him achieve success. This leader invites a healthy debate among stakeholders prior to making key decisions. They channel the discussion toward a mission-driven decision that focuses on customer requirements. Finally, a leader in a high-trust workplace admits errors in judgment and learns from those mistakes.

Leaders at the top level are often faced with divergent stakeholder agendas. How should a leader in balance respond? The direction, we believe, should flow from the organization's mission statement, core values, and business imperatives. A leader in balance is clear on how his or her personal values align with those of the organization. We believe that the ability to establish and articulate *core values* is the core competency.

Many CEOs today promote the establishment of core values and ensure they are published across the organization and are available for the public to read. The recent onslaught of breaches in ethics and executive "perp walks" on national TV has forced companies to at least appear to be concerned about values. A leader in balance is compelled to dig deeper and search her/his personal value system for understanding the boundaries of acceptable behavior. A leader in balance is able to bring a leadership team together to articulate the core values that serve as the foundation for ethical decision making. Once consensus is reached at the top level regarding organizational values, the leader in balance is able to clearly articulate those values across the organization, sharing concrete examples of how everyday dilemmas are dealt with using these values as a compass. A leader in balance behaves in a way that embodies the core values everyday.

President, chairman, and CEO of Eli Lilly and Company, John Lechleiter, had the core values of his organization in mind as he was preparing to take over the helm. He wanted to intentionally build his brand as a leader around the values of the company. He told us,

> It's going to be important that Lilly people hear my expectations around our values as the beacons, the guides of our actions. The brand, in a sense, is a framing of aspirations. The brand articulates our values to the outside world.

Leaders in balance *foster collaboration.* This competency is evidenced when a leader has a clear purpose in mind as it relates to business imperatives each time he brings people together. The leader in balance strives to leverage 100 percent of people's talents 100 percent of the time to achieve the organization's objectives. A driving force for this leader is curiosity—about people, situations, and systems. This leader seeks to understand and tap into people's motivators in order to spark enthusiasm, creativity, and positive outcomes.

The leader in balance has a carefully developed network of employees, customers, and colleagues with whom she/he collaborates to arrive at the best solution for each business problem. A leader in balance understands her/his own strengths and expertise as well as limitations and strives to surround her/himself with people who contribute in ways that are different from her/his ways, yet complementary. We think this leader recognizes talent in others and crafts a leadership-continuity plan to leverage those talents for the survival of the organization. As a foundation for this process, top executives reflect on the core competencies required for success in today's global society. Their role is to place clarity around the behaviors necessary to, in CEO Jack Kraeutler's words, "sit at the table anywhere in the world."

Merely having a list of core competencies on hand, such as managing change, isn't all a leader needs to do. They also need to articulate and model behaviors within each competency. For example, global focus and understanding competency for the leader in balance could be described as follows:

- Demonstrates sensitivity to cultural norms
- Adapts quickly to different cultures
- Transforms knowledge about US markets to global markets
- Tailors decisions to fit the location and culture
- Maintains an awareness of world events that impact the business

A leader in balance is able to share power appropriately. Sharing power does not mean abdication of authority or accountability. Sharing power does not mean hiring one or two colleagues that think and act just like you. Harry Nieman, CEO of Premier Manufacturing Support Services in Cincinnati, Ohio, told us that "sharing power is part of his company's business model." He added that he could not work for an organization that operated under a different model and that a "command and control" approach is a symptom of serious organizational issues. Jack Kraeutler expressed these thoughts: "I should rarely, if ever, demand something because of my position. You have to be among the people in your organization to know their motivations."

Kraeutler's comments are similar to another leader we interviewed, Bob Kohlhepp. Kohlhepp is chairman of Cintas Corporation, headquartered in Cincinnati, Ohio. He says of his current and past role as CEO that "I don't know whether you call it humility or what, but I could care less whether it's my idea. What I'm after is what's the best answer?" Kohlhepp is like other leaders we talked with in that he believes humility is the key to being a leader in balance. He said, "When I was CEO of the company, I used to tell people all of the time that just because I'm the CEO doesn't mean I'm right. Therefore, I want your opinion, and if you think I'm about to do something that doesn't make any sense, say so."

Other leaders we interviewed make intentional choices about sharing power. Don Washkewicz said, "We're a very decentralized organization, so we coined a new kind of term here which, I think, fits Parker. We're a centrally-led decentralized company." This approach has suited Parker well and influenced the company's growth and success in recent years.

In our interview with John Pepper, former CEO of Procter & Gamble and former chairman of the board for the Walt Disney Company, he applauded current Disney CEO Bob Iger's leadership qualities. In John's words, "Bob is very comfortable in his own skin. He is a natural collaborator because he sees the power of all the different parts of Disney coming together around common goals. This is playing out in the business, and other than the quality of the people itself, the biggest strategic advantage that Disney has is the ability to take creative ideas and move them across all the different parts of the company." This is high praise for a company that had, for years, operated in silos that prevented effective communication across divisions.

Another core competency for leaders in balance is *innovation*. An innovative leader creates an environment that is safe for calculated risk taking and models this behavior. An innovative leader is open and receptive to trying new approaches and ideas.

Harry Nieman sponsored an "Innovation Initiative" that uses an Internet portal to connect his employees worldwide in order to share innovations to address business imperatives and problems. This is not merely a sophisticated way for employees to vent. Innovations are reviewed, assessed for alignment with business needs, and implemented. Results of innovations are tracked and measured against strategic objectives.

John Lechleiter at Lilly also talked with us about the importance of innovation. He believes that "promoting innovation and calculated risk-taking promotes employee engagement." He said, "This involves having the courage to act and to take risks, the willingness to accept that not everything is going to work, and a level of comfort with the fact that perfection is not required in every situation."

Innovative leaders leverage existing or potential resources to achieve business objectives. In other words, they find creative ways to utilize 100 percent of their resources 100 percent of the time. For example, leaders in balance not only seek out a qualified, diverse workforce, but they also ensure their employees are actively using their talents and knowledge wisely for their own and the organization's development. Innovative leaders reach out to individuals intentionally as a form of solidarity to connect human needs and wants to the mission and vision of the organization. The result is a higher level of learning across the organization that continually intersects "real-world" constraints and customer needs with the human capital of intellect (see figure 3.1).

Paul Vivek, former CEO of Wipro Technologies and now a respected venture capitalist, shared an interesting story captured on a recent CNET blog. Paul encountered an elephant near Bangalore, India, several years ago. He was curious about why the elephant, which was tied to a small stake in the ground, didn't pull it out and run off. The animal's handler explained that baby elephants tied to similar stakes learn that they can't break free. As they grow older, they don't test the stake again and remain constrained by what should be an obsolete restraint. Paul decided that this could apply to people as well. He decided after that incident that he would not apply artificial constraints to his employees to restrict their creativity and contributions.

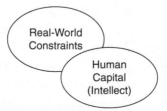

Figure 3.1   Balanced leadership thinking positively leverages human capital.

Experiential learning allows all of us to take classroom concepts and apply them on the job. As Marcus Buckingham and Curt Coffman note in *First, Break All the Rules*,[2] one can have a well of knowledge yet be totally incapable of transferring that knowledge to daily life. The ability to take one's knowledge and use it wisely and appropriately is another critical competency in today's global community. Linda studied textbook Japanese carefully before moving to Japan for three years. Immersion in the culture helped her learn the nuances of Japanese and navigate life among native residents.

A leader in balance learns from life experiences as well as from academic pursuits. As Harry Nieman said during his interview, "The classroom can help me with some things, but not the important things." He believes his constant travel to his customer sites around the world and listening firsthand to their needs teaches him what he needs to know to stay current.

Another leader we interviewed, Dr. Marla Phillips, former Merck quality control officer, is a strong advocate of lifelong learning. She said, "I just don't like not knowing. I love to learn and it has to be lots of diverse things."

Don Washkewicz believes that learning and innovation are major factors in organizational success. He told us, "We want 4 percent of sales coming from things that are either new to the industry or new to the world, not a me-too." He believes that an organization should constantly be improving on their processes. "So the concept is you can always improve, and so the key is your current-state map always turns out to be your future-state map."

The competencies, or behaviors, that we've just described will sound familiar to those of you who have studied "emotional intelligence." In *Resonant Leadership*[3] and *Using Your Emotional Intelligence to Develop Others*,[4] the authors present the concept of emotional intelligence in four primary domains: self-awareness, self-management, social awareness, and interpersonal competence.

For leaders that possess a high degree of self-awareness, using a "gut" sense to guide their decisions is commonplace. These leaders know their strengths and when to use them, as well as their limitations. When a leader understands their boundaries in terms of competency levels, it's an easier choice to bring others into the decision-making process with specific skills and expertise. There is no belief that as leader it is necessary to be all things to all people or carry "false pride." A humble acknowledgment that each individual has talents that can be leveraged opens the door for leaders to let the "right people on the bus," in Jim Collins's terminology in *Good to Great*.[5]

Emotional self-control ensures that leaders are able to engage in objective critical thinking and analysis. Especially in crisis situations, input and behaviors that may be careening out of control need to be managed by the leader in balance. This is the time for a leader to act fluidly adapting to changing situations and obstacles and ready to pounce on opportunities before or as they develop.

Marilyn Shazor said about managing one's emotions, "How I think makes a big difference. Some people are calm and decisive in a crisis and others are affected by their emotions. I don't allow emotions to make decisions for me."

A leader in balance can sense others' emotions, understand them, and be empathetic without letting those emotions negatively affect their ability to function. In order to effectively foster collaboration, a leader in balance must be clear on the dynamics between and among individuals inside and outside the organization. A leader in balance must recognize the needs of others and pose options and approaches that meet those needs in order to crystallize teams and serve as a change catalyst.

A leader in balance employs networks to encourage diversity of thought, innovation, and creativity; to spread influence and power; and organize learning communities that produce disciplined people, thought, and action. Instead of replacing hierarchy, networks can be used to augment it in a balanced manner and to encourage the culture and practice of collaboration.

We believe these competencies and underlying emotional intelligence flow from mindfulness, hope, and compassion. Mindfulness is living in a state of full-conscious awareness of one's self and other people—being present in every moment. Hopeful leaders feel excited about the future and possibilities. Compassionate leaders are in tune with those around them, empathetic to their wants and needs, and motivated by a true concern for others.

In practice, the range of challenges a leader must manage in a balanced manner is highly situational, calling for good judgment, at times intuition, and even wisdom. The notion of balance as conceived in The Kucia Balance Framework[6] means the right chemistry, the right mix, and the right choice at the right time, based upon the situation and the good judgment, intuition, and wisdom of the leader. Balance does not mean "in the middle" or "halfway" or "50/50." An organization as a living system is not under the control of one person or force, but has many influences that necessitate a balanced operation.

An Updated Paradigm Necessitates a Different Set of Behaviors

We believe that the flow of our process under discussion can be depicted as given in figure 3.2. In this next section, we'll share examples of concrete behaviors that more fully demonstrate the competencies described in the first part of this chapter.

A leadership behavior that exemplifies critical thinking is challenging assumptions and engaging in breakthroughs, rather

Figure 3.2 Balanced leadership thinking impacts human capital success.

than accepting the status quo and steering clear of any actions that may involve risk.

Breakthrough actions involve development of a service or product that

- provides a significant customer benefit;
- changes the basis of competition;
- requires a different allocation of resources; and
- creates a new standard or system.

In the late 1990s, Linda was consulting with a medium-sized healthcare facility in the Midwest. The director of human resources was a leader in balance who engaged in breakthrough behaviors on a daily basis. Before other healthcare facilities even considered in-house health fairs as an employee-retention tool, she invited all the organization's health, life, disability, and Employee Assistance Program (EAP) providers to set up booths in the lunchrooms of each facility. Instead of employees being forced to catch time as they could to contact vendors or human resources with questions, they could visit the appropriate vendor booth in their lunchroom during one of their scheduled breaks or before or after work. After this and similar services were implemented, absenteeism and turnover were drastically reduced at a time when other area healthcare institutions were losing quality employees at a rapid pace.

A national nonprofit organization with which Linda consults found that its funding was being cut for the fifth year in a row. As a result, they had to ensure that every dollar was wisely spent to achieve maximum results. The executive director decided to set up benefits-information kiosks throughout the organization and educate the workforce about using the computers in the kiosks. Instead of calling two highly overworked benefits specialists at headquarters, employees could drop by a kiosk at their convenience, type in their employee information and ask questions or make changes, such as address or marital status. After the initial learning curve, the organization found that it could retrain the two benefits specialists to other much-needed positions within the organization.

The leader in balance encourages others to engage in critical thinking by asking what we term "quality dialogue questions." Leaders can model asking these questions in focus groups, one-on-one meetings, or staff meetings. Here are some examples of this type of questions, designed to provoke thought and open dialogue:

> I've always wondered why we...
> I don't think we spend enough time...
> I think we should focus on...
> Our success lies in...
> We are missing a business opportunity with...
> I would like to be able to...
> Everyone knows that _____ but is afraid to talk about it.
> Our meetings would be more effective if...
> I've noticed that...
> Our customers would be happier if...
> I'd like to see more _____ around here.
> I don't fit in here because...

Linda has utilized these questions in several organizations that find themselves in a rut, following the same tired courses of action year after year without truly assessing the purpose of those actions. The leader in balance follows through on these discussions, of course. For example, the last question above is, "I don't fit in here because..." This is often used in the needs assessment stage of a diversity initiative to ascertain whether specific segments of the workforce feel disengaged or disenfranchised. After leading several focus groups in a Midwestern nonprofit agency a couple of years ago, Linda found that people over 40 years of age were feeling disrespected and cut off from the mainstream activities. When she shared this information with the CEO, he immediately began drawing on the expertise of older workers through team leadership opportunities, newsletter editing opportunities, and mentor positions.

In their book, *Riding the Blue Train*,[7] Bart Sayle and Surinder Kumar describe the perfect example of a leader who engages in breakthrough behaviors. In his first major executive meeting after taking over the position of CEO of Wrigley, William Wrigley, Jr., stated in response to a question from one of his executives about the process for getting new initiatives improved, "You already have the approval! That's why you're here. You are the leaders who will set our direction. You don't need to seek approval."

This statement was the catalyst for a major shift in Wrigley's culture and set the stage for empowered executives to reach their potential throughout the worldwide organization.

The leader in balance believes sharing power and encouraging innovation are critical success factors for a long-living organization. The two behaviors we'd like to explore that exemplify this way of thinking are *coaching* and *mentoring*. Often in today's organizations, we hear these two concepts used interchangeably, however, they are not the same.

Coaches do not "tell," they do not "consult." They ask provocative questions, listen with their entire being to the response, and offer tools the other person can select to achieve her/his objective. The most effective coaches we know ask questions that revolve around elements of meaningfulness, such as the following:

- What do you believe in?
- How do you prefer to be treated?
- What types of relationships help you to grow and learn?
- What is your preferred learning style?
- What type of work challenges you?
- How do you prefer to receive feedback and recognition?

Coaching can occur in an afternoon or for one specific project. Mentoring, on the other hand, is long term and involves a different skill set. Linda Gravett was the beneficiary of an excellent mentor during her years as court administrator for the Sixth Circuit Court of Appeals.

The chief clerk of the Sixth Circuit, Lenny Green, established specific objectives for mentoring within the circuit, which covered appellate courts in four states. He decided to craft a process that could be used to recruit and retain talented staff, support leadership continuity, provide networking opportunities, and improve staff morale. He knew at the beginning what success would look like.

Green's next step was to research the competencies that were required for excellent mentors. He had no intention of being a mentor himself, or asking others to fulfill this role unless they possessed (or were willing to acquire) key competencies, such as active listening, creativity, and providing effective feedback. Before a person began a mentor-mentee relationship, they were provided with opportunities to develop these core competencies.

Green served as Gravett's mentor. The first step was to set mutually agreeable expectations for the process, such as meeting times, duration of the official mentor-mentee relationship, and boundaries. Within the court system, Green had plenty of experience in this area, so he was imminently qualified to share ideas about how to succeed in this highly specialized environment. Under his mentorship, Gravett entered a six-year tenure at the court that was productive, fulfilling, and energizing.

A leader in balance knows how to preserve continuity and drive necessary change and learning. There are times in an organization's growth cycle when only small, incremental change is required to ensure success. There are other times when breakthrough behaviors are required to stay ahead of the competition. Times of continuity are those that require organizations to "store energy"; times of change are those that require action, turning stored energy into kinetic energy.

Our observation of successful change initiatives leads us to believe that leaders in balance have some common ways of thinking, being, and acting. Leaders in balance focus on the organization's mission, core values, and strategic objectives. Even when distractions "are buzzing about them," leaders in balance manage the information overload and tune into people, events, and information that help them achieve the organization's key business imperatives.

Leaders in balance focus first on behavior changes in themselves and others, understanding that attitudes may not change immediately. Employees may not fully agree, for instance, that a leader's newly published safety procedures are necessary. The leader wants employees to engage in safe activities first and foremost, regardless of their personal beliefs. Once employees experience a safe, stress-free workplace, their attitude toward following safety procedures is likely to change.

A leader in balance establishes methods to build new competencies in the organization. For example, if the company has decided that one of its key objectives during the coming three years is to expand its marketplace to Southeast Asia, key players will need to expand their language skills so they can function in a different culture, and be well versed in the economy and currency of the target countries.

Washkewicz believes that leaders should view change as a constant: "You think that you have the best concept. Well, it probably isn't always the best. Toyota's been doing this for 50 years."

Bob McDonald, former CEO of Procter & Gamble, said about the change effort in organizations, "You have to work on individuals and you have to work on the organization. Since, in change management, many people work to change the organization, they forget that the organization is a bunch of individuals...and you've got to get individuals to change."

Through the conventions and traditions that comprise an organization's culture, the leader in balance achieves results and effects changes that ensure the company remains cutting edge. The leadership behaviors that are critical during the change effort are envisioning, communicating, motivating, measuring, and retaining change.

Strategic leaders are aware of how events in their environment affect the organization's ability to succeed. Given constant change in a global economy, effective leaders have a vision of how their organization can leverage employees' skills, knowledge, and abilities to take advantage of evolving markets. Visionary leaders regularly ask, "What if we...?" and focus on breakthroughs in technology, services, and products that provide a competitive advantage. From this vision, anchored in core values, flow key result areas or objectives that drive the actions of the leadership team and all employees.

The critical challenge for a leader in balance is finding an effective means to transfer values and a vision for the future from their hearts and minds to the organization's stakeholders. A strategic plan, for instance, is only as effective as the weakest link within the organization, for every employee's talents, abilities, and behaviors must be called upon to implement the plan.

Our experience with top executives who have taken their organizations through significant change efforts is they use a consistent framework for building commitment to change, a framework we call the "PACE" of change (figure 3.3).

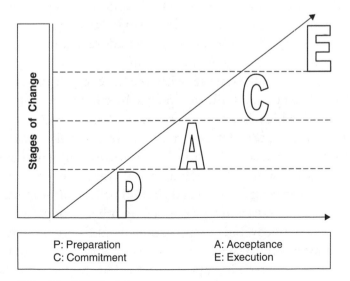

Figure 3.3 The PACE of change.

Using the PACE model shown in figure 3.3, we recommend four phases for communicating and building commitment to change: "Preparation," "Acceptance," "Commitment," and "Execution."

In the *Preparation* phase, the leader in balance lays the groundwork for impending change. For example, let's say that an organization has decided to implement a diversity initiative as part of its strategic plan. Successful implementation may require people to behave differently. Prior to rolling out the initiative, the leader in balance shares information about the world around the organization, such as changes in societal norms, the customer base, and the economy that is necessitating recruiting, developing, and retaining a diverse workforce. This information can be provided in several forms: articles on bulletin boards, on the company website, at companywide meetings, or brown-bag lunch seminars. At this point, there's no "pitch" for people to change; the focus is solely on providing information.

In the second phase, *Acceptance*, the leader in balance brings employees into the change process through solicitation of ideas and suggestions about how potential changes in their work environment might affect them personally, their department, and the company as a whole. The question on most peoples' minds will be, "What will coming changes mean to me and the way I do things?" If this question isn't addressed in the acceptance phase, real change will not occur.

Continuing our example with the diversity initiative, the leader in balance can build acceptance by commissioning a culture audit, which is a needs assessment where issues regarding recruitment, orientation, training, career development, and compensation surface. A culture audit focuses on whether certain employee segments, such as people over 40 years of age, believe they haven't experienced the full benefit of promotional opportunities and training as much as other groups. If issues like this are uncovered, focus groups could be conducted to gain input around ways to ensure every workforce segment is provided with growth opportunities. The leader in balance knows that acceptance of policy changes is more likely to occur if employees have been involved in those changes.

When employees are made aware of specifically how their contributions have affected the organization, the leader in balance has more leverage to establish an environment that motivates people to continue those efforts.

During the *Commitment* phase of the change process, the leader in balance establishes new policies and procedures and then acts on the new ways of behaving in order to serve as a role model. The leader sets and pursues clear objectives, for example, the following diversity goals:

- Expand our recruiting sources to ensure the organization hires more qualified Hispanic and African-American employees by end of the year
- Expand our customer base by midyear to include the 50–65-year-old demographic.

In order to *Execute* change and sustain the momentum, the leader in balance empowers employees to remove artificial barriers and engage in behaviors that support the change effort. For example, if part of a company's diversity initiative is to establish cross-functional process improvement teams that comprise employees at line supervisor, first-line supervisor, and managerial level, the senior person cannot step into the first team meeting and assert him or herself as the boss of everybody. If executives announce that they have an open-door policy to listen and discuss suggestions around expanding a diverse client base, employees cannot be stopped by five assistants and a waiting period of six months before gaining access to those executives.

The leader in balance avoids meetings; keeps his management levels to a minimum; gives his executives financial and creative latitude to make major decisions; and doesn't micromanage. A leader in balance once said, "I've surrounded myself with people who are bright and enthusiastic and don't want a lot of direction. We grew at sixty percent a year for six or seven years. If you don't have this kind of organization, you can't grow like that."

The leader in balance is constantly nurturing change efforts to allow new behaviors to develop, mature, and evolve. Whether the organization has six days or six months to effect change, the leader in balance allows people to move through the four phases in order to fully understand, appreciate, and become involved in the change process.

The leader in balance engages in behaviors that establish and expand networks, as opposed to following hierarchical structures to accomplish organizational objectives. The leader in balance understands when to effect decision making by autocratic methods and when to effect decision making through consensus.

A Reflection

Outdated paradigms, or mental maps about leadership, won't work in today's global society. Critical thinking and analysis, strategic perspective, fostering collaboration, global focus and understanding, sharing power, and innovation are all essential competencies for a leader in balance.

A leader in balance employs networks to encourage diversity of thought and creativity. Networks do not, in all cases, replace existing hierarchies but, rather, enhance and augment this dynamic.

Updated paradigms necessitate updated behaviors for leaders: challenging assumptions, creating breakthrough products and services, engaging in frequent quality dialogues with all stakeholders, and mentoring. These may, on the surface, seem like "soft skills," however, leadership behaviors that minimize conflict, reduce turnover, and enhance productivity directly affect profitability and organizational resiliency.

Chapter 4

The Structure of the Ways of Leaders in Balance

The foundation of our thinking begins with the premise that the leadership required for a living organization in a global society calls for new habits of the mind—a fundamental shift from emphasis on leadership in control to leadership in balance and from a leader's way of behaving to a leader's way of thinking.

In this chapter, we will share "The DNA of Collaboration: The Kucia Balance Framework," which will bring order to understanding the complex range of leadership and organizational challenges. We will begin to answer the question, "What is the role of collaboration for leading change in a global society?"

Paradoxical Challenges

East Informs West Leading to The DNA of Collaboration

Throughout contemporary leadership literature and in the real-world experience of leaders the following challenges prevail:[1]

- Mission versus market
- Continuity versus change
- Collaboration versus competition
- Networks versus hierarchies
- The world of minds (learning driven) versus the world of organizations (bottom-line driven)

- Innovation/creativity versus discipline
- Learner versus teacher
- The virtues of innocence (vulnerable, open to new understanding) versus experience (full of information, knowledge, perhaps even intuition and wisdom)
- Humble versus noble
- Balance versus control

All of these apparent paradoxical challenges are present in the literature and are significant challenges for leaders of the for-profit and the not-for-profit organizations.

However, from the Asian standpoint, continuity and change are neither opposites nor are they in conflict. Instead, as explained by Robert Ballon, S. J., a Jesuit management professor at Sophia University in Tokyo, "from an Asian view, you achieve continuity through change; you continue to survive by changing." Thus, continuity and change are complementary. In like manner, although each of these other pairs of challenges rest at either end of a continuum, neither are they opposites nor are they paradoxes. Each of these pairs represents some dimension of a successful leader's challenge as they learn and grow toward developing their own personal brand—their way of leading. Collaboration offers a means for achieving balance between these elements.

The introduction of this enlightening bit of Eastern thinking informed us, deepened our Western understanding of collaboration, and began to suggest elements of a framework for organization. One can even imagine a kind of harmony to be achieved when these elements are integrated in a balanced manner throughout the leadership, culture, and structures of any organization—for-profit and not-for-profit alike.

This shift in our way of thinking was fortified when Kucia was invited by Procter & Gamble's Bob McDonald, who was chief operating officer at that time, to sit in and observe a closed leadership development session of 50 Procter & Gamble general managers from around the world. In an earlier conversation with Kucia regarding collaboration, McDonald wondered, "What can we learn and what deeper meaning could we derive from the *kanji* characters for collaboration?" McDonald had worked for five years in Japan, so he knew that kanji is a picture language that represents ideas and expresses both the feeling and the actual experience of the idea. At a break, McDonald invited Shinja Okujami, a general manager in Kobe, and Kucia to a flip chart and asked Okujami to write the kanji for collaboration. Shinja quickly drew two kanji characters and offered an enlightening explanation for the concept of collaboration (see figure 4.1).

With quick artistic strokes, Shinja wrote two kanji characters that are the kanji concept for collaboration and then explained their meaning—*root* and *circulate*. This kind of collaboration is an activity that is quiet—below the radar. This idea of collaboration is the quiet, behind-closed-doors work you do before you present the idea or plan to the whole group. You practice this quiet collaboration as you work toward the end product and prepare for change. It is the collaboration on the inside of the organization before you discuss outside. You are laying the groundwork, but do not speak publicly of the ideas before you understand what you are doing with them. Patience, perseverance, and persistence embody the nature of the concept of "root."

根回し *ne ma wa shi*, translated as *root* and *circulate*.

However, root and circulate seemed to lack the transparency that Kucia felt is essential for collaboration, so he asked if there was another kanji interpretation.

Shinja then drew another kanji concept that joined two characters meaning *together* and *power*, and may be interpreted as, "together there is power" or "to be in harmony increases power."

協力 *kyou ryoku*, translated as *together* and *power*.

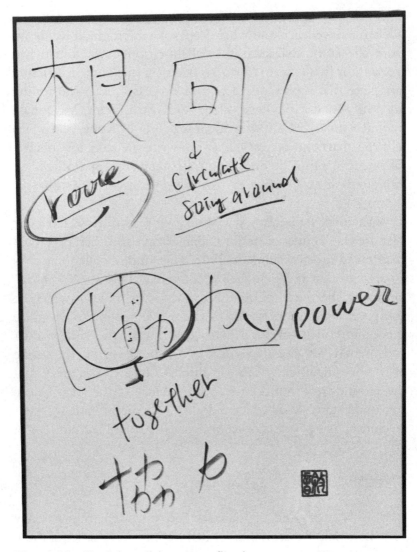

Figure 4.1 Kanji for collaboration—flip chart.

Reflecting upon these kanji concepts, Kucia wondered if there is a Western framework or metaphor that could be created to represent and describe the feeling and actual experience of collaboration that is suggested by these kanji characters.

Kucia also learned that the sequence of these kanji characters adds meaning to the idea of collaboration as well. So after sorting these Asian concepts of collaboration a few different ways, they began to make sense when organized in the following manner:

Root + Circulate = Collaboration

Together + Power = Collaboration

The idea of planning the strategy first—quiet testing of ideas—and then executing the strategy—working together increases power—was logical and rang true. Through this exercise with kanji, Kucia gained a more robust meaning of the notion of collaboration. More importantly, he began to understand two distinct business purposes for collaboration—"to plan strategy" and "to execute strategy."[2]

In pursuit of more order, connection, and purpose, Kucia organized the kanji concepts to arrive at an even richer interpretation: you "bring together at the root" while creating strategy and then you "circulate the power" in the execution of the strategy. Thus, collaboration, written as an equation, looks as depicted in figure 4.2.

The Collaboration Equation

As such, the collaboration equation in figure 4.2 brought some order, even a discipline and more concrete understanding of

Root	+	Circulate	=	Collaboration (Strategy)
+		+		+
Together	+	Power	=	Collaboration (Execution)
↓		↓		↓
Creation of Strategy	+	Execution of Strategy =		Change to address the Challenge

Figure 4.2 The Collaboration Equation.

a purpose for collaboration. The Collaboration Equation suggests a strategic order and the relationship between the stages of collaboration as a purpose-driven means to an end. Further, it suggests that there may be a measurable science to the art of collaboration.

The DNA of Collaboration Discovered: A Balance Framework

The Collaboration Equation suggests a way of understanding the many notions of collaboration. It begins to uncover some order, to define and to simplify collaboration as a means to lead change in a living organization. In order to further develop The Collaboration Equation and apply it to the paradoxical challenges of leadership, Kucia employed the concept of "bricolage," which is an approach to reasoning by analogy that enables one to draw from the experiences and learning of one discipline and apply it to another in order to predict the impact or future outcomes.

We know from de Geus that the way you think of your organization—a machine to make money or a community of talented people—has a fundamental impact on how you lead. We needed something that imagined a living organism, not a machine with someone in charge, flying the plane or driving the bus.

The paired, complementary elements of the Collaboration Equation—*root* and *circulate*, *together* and *power*—suggested to Kucia the structure of the DNA of collaboration and provided a foundation from which to build an analogous model. Reasoning through the analogy of DNA offered a way of organizing, understanding, and thinking about the relationship between the apparently paradoxical challenges of collaboration, that is, market versus mission, continuity versus change, and collaboration versus competition.

The analogous thought process goes like this: collaboration is an essential element in the organic makeup and culture of a long-living organization. Like DNA, collaboration includes complementary elements that must interact in a balanced manner—in the real world, in real time. Balance is as critical to the effective functioning of a living organization as it is to the effective functioning of an organism. The DNA metaphor provides a living image, a simple structure, and a natural order for thinking about the many notions of collaboration: *together* and *power*; *root* and *circulate*. In DNA, one element flows to combine with the other, creating an instinctive balance that is naturally intuited through reflection and action in a fluid manner—like *yin* and *yang*.

By blending this analogous DNA thinking with the order and discipline of The Collaboration Equation, The Kucia Balance Framework emerged as a valuable tool for leaders and their organizations. It organizes the disorderly range of leadership and organizational challenges and behaviors into complementary base pairs, the competencies and capabilities needed for purpose-driven collaboration.

Through The Kucia Balance Framework approach, complementary base pairs such as *mission* ↔ *market, continuity* ↔ *change, collaboration* ↔ *competition, being* ↔ *doing, learning* ↔ *teaching*, and *networks* ↔ *hierarchy* are blended in just the right balance in an integrative manner of *both/and* rather than *either/or*. One is not better or stronger than the other and there is no formula for knowing the right blend for balance. Instead, decisions and actions are based on the situation and the good judgment, intuition, instincts, and wisdom of the leader. Like an accomplished musician or an exceptional athlete, the behavior and the performance becomes part of their nature.

The image of DNA offered a simple conceptual metaphor for the working of "The DNA of Collaboration: The Kucia Balance Framework." It organized and explained the functioning of the complementary "genetic elements" of collaboration and leadership while it also suggested the critical role of balance in both a living organism and a living organization. This thinking was confirmed by Dr. Dorothy Engle, a DNA biologist at Xavier University, in a conversation about the balance framework. Dr. Engle scanned the balance framework and immediately described the very direct relationship between the way DNA actually functions with its complementary base pairs working in balance and the similar logic and flow of the balance framework.

Like DNA, the balance framework organizes base pairs into groupings of competencies and capabilities related to the culture, the structures, the leadership, the change, and the challenge for a collaborative leader. It envisions a personal brand of collaborative leader—an integration of head, heart, and hand—who embodies and models the values and competencies desired throughout the entire organization. As such, the leader is comfortable with not only ambiguity, change, making decisions, and giving direction, but also with distributing power and influence through a diversity of people and ideas.

As depicted by the framework, the collaborative leader uses good judgment and, oftentimes, intuition to skillfully balance the influence of competition (bottom-line driven) with collaboration (purpose driven). The collaborative leader balances teaching (knowing and challenging) with learning (curious and reflecting) and reliance on the hierarchy (dependence) with the network (interdependence). Through this very intentional preference for balance instead of control, the collaborative leader is able to meet the challenges (complex or linear) and changes (transformational or incremental) needed to accomplish the mission and goals of the organization whose culture, structures, and leadership are purposefully connected.

Diagrammed, these complementary base pairs form The Kucia Balance Framework shown in figure 4.3.

The *power* side of the framework represents the traditional Western, industrial, command-and-control hierarchy whose strategies have been strongly influenced by Sun Tzu's *The Art of War*[3] and the material martial arts. Organized for competition and bottom-line driven, this philosophy is based upon the opposition of forces—fighting and war—with a clear strategic focus on how to win. The leader is the central authority, the power, the

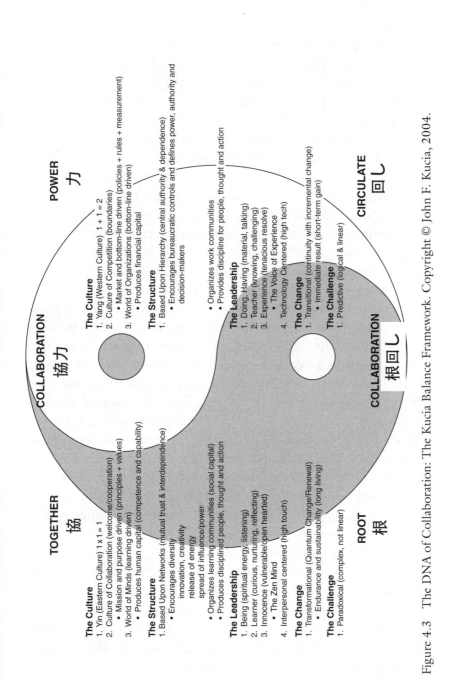

Figure 4.3 The DNA of Collaboration: The Kucia Balance Framework. Copyright © John F. Kucia, 2004.

voice of experience, the teacher. The hierarchy is a familiar structure and strategy because it is the way things have been done for centuries. Today's leaders have studied and learned how to work this hierarchical, command-and-control system and it has been successful. We all know leaders who are very skilled, but comfortable *only* with this approach to leading an organization; they are very uncomfortable with the idea of collaboration.

The *together* side of the framework represents an Eastern, more collaborative approach to leadership strongly influenced by Morihei Ueshiba's *The Art of Peace*[4] and the spiritual martial arts. Relationships and influence become the *power* factor. The strategic focus is not on how to win, but on how to emerge victorious in any situation. This approach takes a view from a higher level and of the totality—it never seeks to make enemies, follows natural principles, and seeks to harmonize and develop techniques of harmony rather than contention.

Organized around networks that reach across organizational boundaries, it calls for leaders charged with more responsibility than authority, to be able to successfully work across the matrix. Consequently, this calls for leaders who bring a way of being, a spiritual energy, listening, learning, and reflection—all very different competencies from the command-and-control authority. Leaders who are uncomfortable with command and control think of collaboration as consensus building and, therefore, seek to gain consensus before making a decision. There are very few leaders who have mastered the kind of leading as described on the together side of the framework.

Here is the way The Kucia Balance Framework is interpreted.

On the *power* side, the "challenge" represents the type of issue a leader is addressing. If the leader has a situation in which the problem, opportunity, or work to be accomplished is clear and the solution can be discovered and executed through some transitional or incremental change within the ordinary structures of the organization, that situation would likely draw more on the traditional hierarchy and those capabilities and competencies of the leader and the culture. For example, one of Gravett's clients, a CEO, envisioned a move into the realm of e-commerce. The CEO is also chief technical officer of this family-owned business. It's his leadership vision and traditional hierarchy of web developers that report to him that can carry out this vision once it's articulated clearly and concisely.

In contrast, along the *together* side of the balance framework, a leader would address a challenge that is more complex in which the problem, opportunity, or solution, its parts and their interdependence, are difficult to grasp. In situations where no one person or division of the organization can possibly develop the answer, the solution requires a creative, diverse network of people and thinking to bring about transformative or quantum change. This situation would likely draw upon the network and those elements of the leader and the culture described along the *together* side of the framework. The qualities, behaviors, values, and elements listed under the culture also apply to the leader, since the leader reflects the image, behavior, and priorities of the organization. In order to fully execute the CEO's vision mentioned in the previous example, he will need to build a culture of innovation, trust, and risk taking that will require positive collaboration from all staff.

To reemphasize this important concept, in practice, the range of challenges a leader must manage in a balanced manner is highly situational calling for good judgment and, at times, intuition, instincts, and even wisdom. Balance between the together and power perspectives of the balance framework is key to success—a collaborative mind and collaborative action. Collaboration is done well when it blends just the right balance of these elements, the DNA of collaboration, in an integrative manner of *both/and* rather than *either/or*. The notion of balance as conceived in the framework means the right chemistry, the right mix and choice, at the right time, based upon the situation and the good judgment, intuition, and wisdom of the leader. Balance does not mean in the middle, halfway, or 50/50. An organization, as a living system, is not under the control of one person or force, but has many influences that necessitate a balanced approach.

Dr. Engle explained the way DNA functions, which helped us understand even better the analogous application to the balance framework. She stated,

> The DNA molecule serves well as a metaphor for a cell, an individual, or a living organization. This cell stores information, establishing the genetic code determining the tendencies for a living organism. DNA houses the information and instructions to perform work and establishes the basic operating conditions under which a living organism works. Thus, DNA represents a set of values inherent in the nature or the culture of an organism. DNA can be changed but, to change, it first requires environmental pressure to change, followed by much effort.

For the real DNA molecule to do its work, it must have both sides of the double helix, its base pairs, working in complementary balance. Although all cells in an organism have the same DNA, they do not use all base pairs all the time. Instead, they use the base pairs needed to accomplish the work at that period in time and those specific to their function. By analogy, then, the DNA molecule possesses all the information, instructions, and values—the genetic code of the organism. When a leader makes choices and creates the strategy for the organization, they decide which complementary base pairs of DNA are needed in that particular situation to accomplish something, solve a problem, or seize an opportunity.

The figures 4.4, 4.5, and 4.6 illustrate The DNA of collaboration as a metaphor for the functioning of a collaborative leader in a living organization.

The figure 4.4 reinterprets The Kucia Balance Framework as a DNA ladder—the double helix before it is twisted. In this image, the rails of the ladder represent the collaboration equation—the foundations for the strategy and execution of collaboration: *together* and *root, power* and *circulate*. The rungs of the ladder represent the interdependent, complementary base pairs, the genetic competencies and capabilities for collaboration. Both the rails and the rungs are necessary in the culture, the structures, and the leadership in order to address the challenges of change in a living organization.

The figure 4.5 depicts the classic double helix with its simple and elegant gently twisting ladder visually suggesting the dynamic synergy of balance and power created when these elements join together.

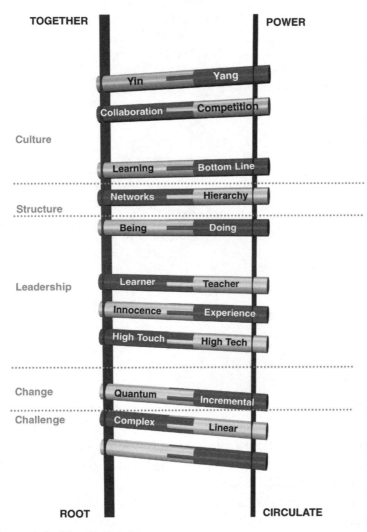

Figure 4.4   The DNA ladder.

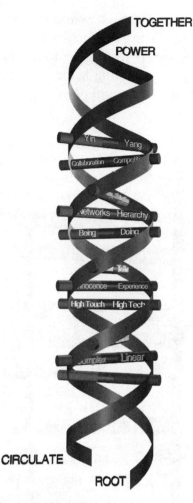

Figure 4.5 The classic double helix twisted.

The figure 4.6 provides a closer view of the interdependent union of these complementary pairs. Just as the yin and yang complement and flow from and into one another, so do the forces of competition and collaboration and so on flow throughout the balance framework.

The capacity to collaborate is a building block of organizational competency that can be learned, developed, or "engineered" in a leader's organization through a focused purpose,

Figure 4.6   A closer view of interdependence—Yin and Yang.

intentional effort, and measurement of progress over a period of time. A different kind of leader and a different way of thinking—a shift in thinking—are required to accomplish this kind of change. This personal brand of leader looks to mission, purpose, principles, and values—the *together* side of The Kucia Balance Framework—as the primary guides for decision making and action. This leader balances these with policies, rules, and objective measurements—the *power* side of The Kucia Balance Framework.[5]

A Reflection

To tie things together in this chapter, Japanese kanji has provided us with a deeper understanding of the idea of collaboration. It has allowed us to envision the actual work of collaboration. We have learned from kanji two ways to depict and understand collaboration—*root* and *circulate* and *together* and *power*—English words we intellectually understand, but kanji combines these concepts to describe the actual experience of collaboration. They describe real situations prompting reflection and learning that build upon one another. These lessons are embedded with wisdom within the understanding of the word. By combining these concepts, we define a purpose and an order for two distinct, yet interdependent, levels of collaboration in the Collaboration Equation. We bring together at the root while creating strategy and, then, we circulate power in the execution of the strategy—a simple understanding of the collaborative way of leading.

Upon further reflection offered by Ellen Mazza, an American woman fluent in Japanese and a student of Japanese culture and music,

> *Kyouryoku* 協力 can be visualized as a group standing together in agreement and moving together in action. *Kyouryoku* is a physical, visibly clear gesture of the cooperation in collaboration. On the contrary, *nemawashi* 根回し can be conceptualized as a behind-the-scenes collaboration where the groundwork and plans are being made and checked quietly and without overt gestures of collaboration.[6] Similar to the biological reality of DNA below our skin, *nemawashi* is a spiritual/metaphysical reality that is subconsciously working in our body. Much like the DNA in our genes, we do not often think about *nemawashi* flowing through our brain and into our actions, ultimately providing immeasurable amounts of power and energy. In the full etymology of *nemawashi* and its parts in relation to The Kucia Balance Framework, we find patience, perseverance, and persistence to be integral parts and sources of power in the quiet side of the balance framework.
>
> *Nemawashi* is not merely laying the groundwork for collaboration. It is the force, the spirit of patience and persistence in humans that makes collaboration possible. The *root* in The Kucia Balance Framework means having a deep understanding of one's spirit, will power, temper, patience, and ability to persevere. The deeper a leader understands and is conscious of these elements about one's self, the greater the leader will be.

It is at the superficial level that most analogous references to individual and corporate DNA end—a set of values that are key to the individual or organization and the way business is conducted. However, The Kucia Balance Framework applies this thinking broader and deeper into the culture and structure of organizations and to the thinking and being of their leaders. Thus, we have the following valuable tool to plumb deeper into a leader's way of thinking, understanding, and being, which gives rise to her/his judgment and paves the way for the choices and behavior of a leader in balance—one able to lead a long-living organization in the twenty-first-century global society.

- A person, a master teacher and a master learner who thinks critically and reflectively with the *head of a strategist*, able to lead an organization that has the ability to learn (sensitive to the environment) and govern its own growth and evolution (wise use of resources)
- A person who nurtures the heart and soul of the organization and its individuals and makes choices and decisions with a *moral and ethical heart*, able to lead an organization that has the ability to build community and a persona for itself (cohesion and identity)
- A person who first chooses to serve others through a higher purpose and executes strategy with the *hand of a collaborative leader*, able to lead an organization that has the ability to build constructive relationships with other entities within and outside (tolerance and decentralization)

In chapter 5, we will begin to see how the concepts of leadership in balance are intentionally applied in corporations, universities, and other nonprofits.

Chapter 5

The Power of Leadership in Balance: The Connection to an Organization's Survival

We've described the ways of thinking of a leader in balance and outlined critical competencies and behaviors that evolve from these ways of thinking. We believe it is just as important to consider the power these behaviors possess to ensure an organization's survival. In this chapter, we'll focus on the positive impact a leader in balance can have on organizational resiliency—the ability to bend and bounce back from hardship.

Resilient organizations such as Procter & Gamble, Xavier University, Meridian Diagnostics, Parker Hannifin, and Premier Manufacturing Support Services share some common characteristics:

- An ethical decision-making framework—an approach toward making high-integrity decisions across an organization that is clearly articulated internally and externally
- A culture of high trust
- A balance between risk and tradition (respect for possibilities versus respect for history)
- The ability to engage in continuous change

These shared characteristics don't just occur serendipitously—they are the intentional choice of leaders in balance. In figure 5.3, Model for Resiliency, you will see specific examples of how a leader in balance can strengthen an organization.

Harry Nieman has taken purposeful steps over the past few years to build a strong framework for ethical decision making. The basis for the framework is a code of ethics developed by the executive team with input from staff across the organization. Linda Gravett was called upon to guide the leadership team through the process of building an ethical decision-making framework that could be communicated and implemented across the organization. Candid discussions took place within the team meetings that surfaced everyday ethical dilemmas faced by employees throughout the international organization. During these discussions, Niemen did not preach; he did not tell his executives what to do. He brought discussions back to the company's code of ethics and core values and asked, "What's the appropriate response to this issue based on our stated values?"

While competitor companies vacillated about issues such as accepting gifts from vendors, sending the message to the global community that their moral compass was not firmly set, Premier Manufacturing employees around the world consistently follow their stated principles. The message that Premier operates within ethical guidelines was sent and received and their customer base has grown.

Besides following the basic code of ethics, the employees have a decision-making framework that involves asking themselves the following key questions when faced with an ethical dilemma:

• Does this decision support our organization's core values?
• Am I committed enough to this decision to stake my job on it?
• Does this decision support the interests of our organization's stakeholders?
• Will my decision build or tear down trust?
• Is the decision clearly based on facts?

John Lechleiter of Eli Lilly and Company believes that integrity and excellence are integral, foundational aspects of leadership. He told the authors that he and his team talk a great deal about these characteristics at his company and they form a component of the Lilly brand.

It's difficult for a leader to distribute a survey like the Trust Audit in figure 5.1 because the results may or may not be positive. However, the director of aviation for a Gravett client airport did just that and asked employees to be completely candid. The response rate was high—employees had been waiting a long time for this opportunity to vent! The trust level across the organization at that time was low. People in key positions

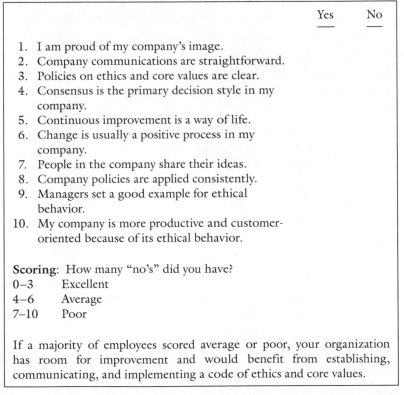

	Yes	No
1. I am proud of my company's image.		
2. Company communications are straightforward.		
3. Policies on ethics and core values are clear.		
4. Consensus is the primary decision style in my company.		
5. Continuous improvement is a way of life.		
6. Change is usually a positive process in my company.		
7. People in the company share their ideas.		
8. Company policies are applied consistently.		
9. Managers set a good example for ethical behavior.		
10. My company is more productive and customer-oriented because of its ethical behavior.		

Scoring: How many "no's" did you have?
0–3	Excellent
4–6	Average
7–10	Poor

If a majority of employees scored average or poor, your organization has room for improvement and would benefit from establishing, communicating, and implementing a code of ethics and core values.

Figure 5.1 Trust Audit: Do you have a high-trust organization? Copyright © Gravett and Associates, 2002.

had slowly been leaving over the previous three or four years. The Trust Audit helped the aviation director understand some of the reasons for this devastating turnover.

Rather than ignore the negative responses or attribute the negativity to "bad attitudes," the director examined his leadership style. He had to admit that he was often autocratic in his decision-making style, leaving no room for input from employees or managers. He was often hesitant to share bad news such as carrier rate increases that might cause employees concern. Of course, this lack of sharing more often than not caused worry and anxiety because employees heard bad news from newspaper or TV reports.

The director decided to balance "telling" with "guiding" and to move toward participative decision making. He initiated employee meetings across the organization and met with these groups in person to share the results of the Trust Audit. He solicited their ideas to make communications more effective and decisions more transparent. Gravett assisted by providing the following quality dialogue questions, discussed in chapter 3, to start meaningful discussions:

- I've always wondered why we...
- I don't think we spend enough time...
- I think we should focus on...
- Our success lies in...
- I would like to be able to...
- Our customers would be happier if...
- I'd like to see more _____ around here.

Based on input he received from these meetings, the director developed an action plan that involved managers and employees. He went back to his workforce for additional input. He asked for employees' support, and they gave it. The airport has seen positive results in terms of work quality, customer satisfaction, and employee job satisfaction and retention. Today, the organization is thriving, with low employee turnover.

Bob Castellini of the Castellini Company summed up the integrity issue very succinctly in our interview when he said, "I used to tell all my produce salesmen, 'Don't ever lie to a customer or a supplier.' Integrity is extremely important, but let's even be more practical. These guys are on the phone all day long, so if they play loosely with the truth on a Monday, how do they remember that on a Friday?" This way of thinking paid off for Castellini. He grew the family produce business into a national company in the years he was at the helm.

The leader in balance demonstrates a curiosity about possibilities, yet values a historical perspective in order to maintain continuity. This approach is also depicted in the Model for Resiliency (figure 5.3). Taken to its extreme, openness to alternatives can result in a leader who cannot remove "rose-colored glasses" about each and every potential venture, product, or employee who crosses her/his path. On the other hand, large and unwieldy organizations that emphasize tradition to the exclusion of positive change will find they are operating on denial and nostalgia. These organizations will lose their competitive edge and talented employees won't seek them out.

The leader in balance ritualizes ingenuity. They encourage others to improve solutions when traditional methods simply won't work. This results in an innovation meritocracy, where excellent ideas prevail, regardless of the source. UPS, for instance, considers improvisation to be a core competency. Its leaders empower employees to do whatever is necessary to deliver packages on time. CEO Mike Eskew has said, "If that means they need to improvise, they improvise. Otherwise, we just couldn't do what we do every day."[1]

In order to drive and sustain change, every organization needs revolutionaries—people who challenge the status quo, seek excellence, and think in terms of infinite possibilities. The leader in balance promotes a culture that balances healthy optimism and intelligent skepticism depicted in figure 5.2.

Figure 5.2   Balancing tradition with potential.

Note in this model, the balance point is not at the line's center. That's because balance is not always 50 percent of one behavior and 50 percent of another. There are times in an organization's life cycle when a leader must foster innovation and collaboration and take calculated risks that feel uncomfortable. In order to engage in breakthrough thinking that results in competitive advantage, however, the right balance might be 60 percent optimism and 40 percent skepticism. Balance, then, is at the core of one's thinking and concomitant behaviors, not in the middle.

Often, organizational leaders move toward closure after decisions are made and healthy, positive change becomes a massive effort. Resilient organizations are evolving organizations. Just as one positive change is in place, another iteration of change begins. This process can go on indefinitely. In other words,

Resiliency = Change = Infinity

Don Washkewicz spoke of this dynamic often during our interview with him. He resonated to the approach Toyota has used for the past 50 years:

> They say we've about perfected this now, so now we're going to execute on it and we're going to put it in place; we're going to put this cell in place; we're going to move the equipment; we're going to do whatever. That turns out to be your future-state map and that's what you're executing. As soon as you do that, what do you do now? You start your new value-stream map because you can always improve on everything you're doing.

Parker Hannifin is a $10 billion company in terms of revenues with 900,000 product offerings.

A resilient organization has systems and processes that flow with a dynamic, fluid energy. Gravett has learned the importance of this energy from practicing the martial arts and *T'ai Chi*. Each *kada* (set of movements) that a T'ai Chi student performs must begin by "calling in the chi" or energy. This energy is necessary to move quickly, change direction, and ward off opponents. Such is the case with leaders in resilient organizations. Each day, the leader in balance must mentally summon energy and receptivity to ideas to create, adapt, and thwart negative forces from inside and outside the organization.

The leaders we interviewed encourage innovation and promote an environment ripe for calculated risk taking. Bob McDonald is a master of this. He told us,

> I spend a lot of my time trying to figure out what capabilities we need to build to win in the future and also doing the training of people in order to get them there. That requires us to place some bets because you don't necessarily know for sure what capability you need in the future.

McDonald is not only cognizant of his need to be innovative and take calculated risk—he proactively sets the stage for quality dialogue around what's fresh and new:

> We get groups of people together to work against specific mission elements. As I'm doing that, I'm also trying to be aware that that mission is for this year. I also have to worry about next year's mission and the mission five years from now which may be different, and so I'm looking for trends in what I'm doing to give me some illumination on what capability we'll need in the future and how things will change in the future.

A Reflection

We believe that leaders in balance establish an intentional design for organizational resiliency. A model we propose is depicted in figure 5.3.

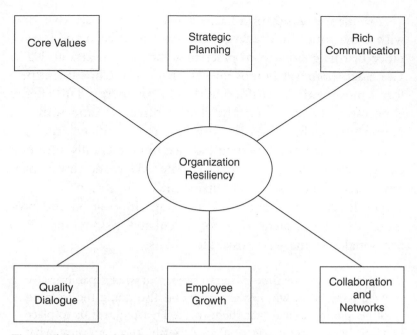

Figure 5.3   Model for Resiliency.

The leader in balance is clear on her/his core values and is able to articulate them throughout the organization. The leaders we interviewed had a similar response to the question "how do you know that individuals incorporate the organization's core values in their day to day work?" "By observation," was the reply given most often.

Communications are transparent and rich, which means they are often face-to-face. Face-to-face communication minimizes the risk that filters, such as education, culture, gender, age, or personality differences, can bring and diminish the message. The leader in balance dedicates energy to exploring new strategic options *and* pursuing efficiency. One eye is on the vision and the other is on ensuring that products and services exceed customer expectations.

The leader in balance builds networks and shares power ensuring participative and collective decision making. Even when a final decision has to be made, this leader solicits and actively listens to input from stakeholders throughout the organization. In her own organization, Gravett does this by intentionally sitting at the middle of the table during meetings with staff rather than at the head of the table. When she poses a question for discussion, she doesn't share her own opinion until everyone else in the room has expressed theirs.

The result of these efforts is a resilient organization that responds successfully to continuous change without destructive turmoil. To sustain this resiliency, employees are provided with the opportunity for continuous growth and development of the competencies necessary to ensure organizational success.

Chapter 6

New Habits of the Mind:
The Ways of a Leader in Balance

A leader is a *brand* and like a brand, leaders and their organizations are built from the inside out. When we say, "I like the way that person thinks," we make a judgment about something broader than a style of leadership, more than a set of leadership characteristics and behaviors, and deeper than a way of leading. We judge the way a person thinks. This goes well beyond a style or approach; it's more telling and more robust. It is about a leader's way of seeing, thinking, and interpreting meaning for their organization—each at the foundation of what's inside a leader. This leader embodies the brand promise and its values and, as such, sets the tone and direction for the organization.

Becoming a leader in balance calls for two essential new habits of the mind—fundamental shifts in ways of thinking—a shift from emphasis on control to balance and from ways of behaving to ways of thinking. Rather than teaching the external techniques of how to move your mouth (ways of speaking) or move your body (ways of behaving), leaders in balance concentrate attention on the inside first—how to move your mind with different ways of thinking, seeing, and understanding—the factors that establish the foundation and pave the way for a leader's decisions and subsequent actions.

To enrich our thinking about leaders in balance with real experiences, Kucia asked leaders to reflect on the topic of collaboration and leadership, and individual and organizational learning and change. He then listened for common patterns in their ways of thinking, seeing, and understanding situations. He was listening carefully to leader's responses looking to integrate and organize the way leaders think and reflect across the image of a leader in balance—a fully integrated person who is simultaneously a person who is a critical thinker and reflective strategist (head); is a moral and ethical builder of trust (heart); and who shares power and authority and encourages innovation (hand).

Creating this image of an individual who thinks with the *head of a strategist*, makes choices with a *moral and ethical heart*, and leads with the *hand of a collaborative leader* may seem lofty and is rarely found, but given the challenging role of leadership today, Kucia believes setting high standards and thinking in terms of the ideal is both warranted and demanded by constituencies around the globe.

Kucia also listened for an awareness of the leader as brand and the importance of trust as they shared and explored the ideas, observations, and challenges from an intellectual and experiential perspective that have led them to their own evolving personal brand of leadership.

The Ways of Thinking of Leaders in Balance: A Brand of Collaborative Leader

"The leader's way of seeing things has special weight. Leaders manage meaning for one group, offering a way to interpret or make sense of and so react emotionally to a given situation," according to the authors of *Primal Leadership: Learning to Lead with Emotional Intelligence*.[1] Leadership in balance is not a *style* of leadership; rather it is leadership with a *personal style*. Leadership in balance is more than a set of leadership characteristics and behaviors and it is deeper than a way of leading. Instead, leadership in balance is a way of thinking, a way of understanding and being that forms the foundation for a leader's decisions and actions. A leader in balance is a robust brand of leader best suited for guiding a living organization of talented people in a contemporary, global, and ever-changing world. Just as a brand is built from the inside out, so are collaborative leaders and their organizations. This brand of leader sets the tone that permeates the culture deep into the organization and beyond. This brand of leader truly believes that the challenges of change are no longer adequately addressed by leadership in control, but by a leader in balance who practices the following "Eight Ways of Thinking":

1. *Approaches leadership as a relationship not a position*
   - Shows respect for people by listening closely
   - Creates bonds of friendship and a sense of camaraderie
   - Engenders a sense of humility balanced with enormous organizational ego
   - Creates loyalty to the institution rather than to self, which builds organizational capability
   - Understands that leadership is more than one person can accomplish alone
   - Needs help and admits mistakes
   - Realizes the competitive advantage of harnessing the power of interdependence and purpose-driven collaboration as a way of proceeding as a leader and as an organization
   - Understands the operative word is leadership, not collaboration
2. *Understands that the leader embodies the brand promise*
   - Is both noble and humble and embodies the values and principles of the organization
   - Sets the tone by what is done and valued
   - Understands that trust is the essential foundation for collaboration balanced with normal instincts for competition
   - Addresses issues with honesty, trust, integrity, respect, and affection for the dignity of others
   - Brings social and emotional intelligence to leadership
   - Has a transparent way of making decisions with personal behavior that nurtures trust
   - Models and communicates a set of expectations and preferences for behavior of other leaders throughout the organization beginning at the top
   - Understands that many people inside and outside the organization derive their relationship with the institution through their real or perceived image of the leader

3. *Is motivated by a higher purpose—a mission—and believes that mission drives the numbers*
   - Focuses attention on purpose, mission, and values of the institution to raise people's motivation above personal interest to serve society
   - Realizes that sole focus on the bottom line may lead to short-term thinking and not long-term life
   - Understands that interdependence and collaboration are essential to accomplish the purpose and mission in any organization
   - Energetically collaborates inside the organization so they can successfully compete outside
   - Understands that if we accomplish the mission we make a lot of money

4. *Understands collaboration must have a business purpose*
   - Is a pragmatist—you can't get good results if you can't collaborate
   - Demonstrates positive regard for collaboration because of successful experiences
   - Gains personal maturity and new insights
   - Believes collaboration, cooperation, and interdependence are a business and cultural necessity
   - Knows that collaboration is hard work—harder than command and control—and is not the slow, soft side of management. Instead, it requires courage, commitment, and, sometimes, conflict as disagreement to differentiate the nature of a problem or a solution
   - Understands the two parts of purpose-driven collaboration as a means to an end: (a) to reach better decisions and to implement them better; and (b) to get the right answer and to get it executed
   - Believes that the reasons for collaborating are to accomplish something, to solve a problem, to get something done, and to understand that results are the reason to collaborate

5. *Thinks outside of the pyramid in order to share power and spread leadership, authority, and responsibility throughout the organization*
   - Balances the present reality with movement toward the future reality and ponders the future shape and structure of the organization

- Envisions a new structure—an internal network of creative people collaborating on issues that require more learning, entrepreneurial, creative, and innovative action. This produces individual and organizational growth and change, new competencies, disciplined people, thought and action, and a new network of influence, power, and learning that augments the hierarchy
- Has the skill and judgment—intuition and instinct—to know how and when to unify and orchestrate the network and hierarchy
- Is fluid in the situation and fluid in the decision

6. *Believes teaching and leadership have a great deal in common*
   - Is both a teacher and leader which is accomplished by (a) asking hard questions and stimulating learning in search of reality and truth, and (b) which leads to setting the right course and creating the right strategy in a disciplined, deliberate, and intentional manner.
   - Knows a master teacher must be a master learner who listens, who observes, who is curious, who admits to not having all the answers, and who is open to learning and therefore somewhat vulnerable
   - Encourages learning through coaching
   - Learns in the real world rather than intellectualizing

7. *Understands that at the center of collaboration is a personal comfort with valuing the diversity of people, ideas, and ways of thinking*
   - Understands this requires a level of individual and organizational cultural competence
   - Allows people to learn, grow, and trust by spending time listening and getting to know one another in an ad hoc collaborative community—a powerful concept, a network of collaborative leadership
   - Is culturally competent and comfortable with a diversity of ideas, people, gender, ethnicity, race, and nationality
   - Believes diversity is an enormously strengthening factor—getting the right people and right balance
   - Understands that comfort and trust of diversity gives more potential to include others

8. *Believes that the challenge of leading change is not about leadership in control, but leadership in balance*
   - Believes that collaboration is a means to leadership in balance

- Believes that a collaborative leader is an integrated person, not a user of techniques or adopter of styles
- Is comfortable with ambiguity and change, with giving direction and making decisions
- Blends the use of data with good judgment and, oftentimes, intuition, instincts, and wisdom to skillfully balance the forces of competition (bottom-line driven) collaboration (purpose driven), teaching (knowing and challenging) learning (curious and reflecting), and the hierarchy (dependence) with the network (interdependence) to meet the challenges (complex or linear) and changes (transformational or incremental) needed to accomplish the leadership challenge at hand.

The Eight Ways of Thinking, when applied to the paradoxical, real-world challenges that are addressed in chapter 4, capture the leadership challenges that must be managed in a balanced manner as they are organized and brought to life in The Kucia Balance Framework. With a fuller understanding of the new habits of mind, we shift our emphasis from ways of behaving "to ways of thinking," and we look again to Asian wisdom for some clues to help us understand the shift from control to balance.

Understanding the Power of Balance: East Informs West

In chapter 4, we discussed the structure of the ways of leadership and highlighted the need for good judgment, intuition, and even wisdom in order to arrive at a balance between the *together* and *power* dimensions of the balance framework. So, what more can we learn about this concept of balance that is so critical to the thinking and being of a leader in balance?

In William R. Torbert's 1991, *The Power of Balance*, he approached his study of the use of power and leadership from an oblique direction as he flipped the balance of power and dug deeply into the power of balance, a concept that is at the very foundation of our book. We believe that the challenges of leading change in the twenty-first century are not about leadership in control, but leadership in balance. Torbert develops seven separate archetypes that key on leadership behaviors ranging from the opportunist and the diplomat to the strategist and the magician. Torbert describes the intellectual power of balance to include:

> the executive capacity to think on one's feet in the midst of crisis. It includes the moral capacity to act with integrity and compassion in time of pressure, adversity, turbulence, and transformation. It includes the strategic capacity to weave all that one knows, all that one intuits, and all that one neglects, into actions that reverberate positively on all time horizons. It includes the visionary capacity to see what one does not see—the visionary capacity to challenge the assumptions of one's current way of seeing and thinking, the visionary capacity to see other perspectives and to see through transformations in one's own perspective.[2]

Although Kucia agreed with Torbert's intellectual capacities, he wanted to know more about how these are accomplished. So he drilled down to discover more dimensions and mental models and tools that enable us to recognize the ways of such a leader. Thus, The Eight Ways of Thinking of a leader in balance and The Kucia Balance Framework emerged to bring some order and purpose to the leadership behaviors and competencies a leader must master in order to successfully address the challenges and change required to accomplish the mission and goals of a long-living organization in a twenty-first-century society.

To gain more insight into the concept of balance, an essential dimension of leadership in balance, we again pursued what can be learned from the wisdom of Asian thinking and the Japanese kanji characters for balance. In Thomas Cleary's *The Book of Balance and Harmony*,[3] he offers a simple and practical understanding and application of balance to a real-time leadership situation when he observes:

> When emotions have not yet emerged, that is called *balance*; when they are active yet in proportion that is called

harmony. If one can be balanced and harmonious in one's self then that person is fundamentally clear and aware, awake in quietude, accurate in action, thus one can respond to the endless changes in the world.

So, balance and harmony, openness and awareness, and calmness and clarity begin to define the mindful, intentional ways of being of a leader in balance. Then kanji provides an additional, richer dimension of experience that describes balance. Where words are used to describe an idea, kanji offers pictures to describe a situation as follows:

The Japanese kanji *tsuriai* (釣合) is a noun for *balance* and is translated as *tsuri* (釣), which means fishing/angling, and *ai* (合), which means be together/fit/join. This is *the state of being in balance* (釣合).

The Japanese kanji *tsuri awaseru* (釣合せる) is the verb for *to balance* and combines *tsuri* (釣), which means fishing/angling, and *awaseru* (合せる), which means to tune in, compare and join together, which is the *act* of listening in a fluid, real-time motion. Another way of expressing this is that *balance* is accomplished by tuning in and adjusting and angling where necessary. Yet another way of envisioning this is to be fluid in the moment, to be like water flowing past obstacles, creating a path of least resistance, proceeding in a manner of leading in balance.

One additional concept of balance is drawn from the principles of *Aikido* (合気道), a modern martial art first described in the explanation of the balance framework in chapter 4. You will recall that the strategy of the traditional command-and-control hierarchy is strongly influenced by Sun Tzu's *The Art of War*[4] and the material martial arts. Organized for competition, this philosophy, this way of thinking, is based upon the opposition of forces—fighting and war with a clear, strategic focus on how to win. The leader is the central authority, the source of power.

As a balance to art of war thinking, we can learn new thinking from Kisshomaru Ueshiba's *Spirit of Aikido*,[5] which introduces us to a more collaborative approach to leadership where relationships and influence become the *power* factor. *Aikido*, the spiritual martial art of peace describes *action* (centered, intuitive, natural) in a (clear-minded) response to an external stimulus or threat. "In movement, the person becomes like a spinning top, stable in the center (achieving unity of mind and body), and never losing balance." Morihei Ueshiba, in his book *The Art of Peace*,[6] makes a valuable observation about his "martial art of peace" when he says, "It is not about the footwork of a martial art technique. I'm not teaching you how to move your feet; I'm teaching you how to move your mind." These are new habits of the mind—a shift in ways of thinking, understanding, and being. This way of leading is always centered—balanced in stillness and movement—balanced in reflection and action.

Considered as one, these are the mindful, intentional ways of being that influence the thinking and inform and animate the actions of a leader in balance:

1. Mindful and intentional about achieving balance and harmony, openness and awareness, and calmness and clarity
2. Fluid in the moment, like water, flowing past obstacles, creating a path of least resistance proceeding in a manner of leading in balance
3. *Listening* and *acting* and *balancing* in a fluid real-time motion
4. *Tuning in* and *adjusting* and *angling* where need be
5. *Taking action* (centered, intuitive, natural) in clear-minded response to external stimuli or threats
6. Like a spinning top, stable in the center (a unity of mind and body) and never losing balance
7. Always centered—balanced in stillness and movement— balanced in reflection and action

Bob McDonald described a "crouching tiger," full of quiet calm and confidence, ready to pounce on the next opportunity to move his organization further in one of their market niches. Bob doesn't have to have a flurry of activity around him. He just focuses on the right activities at the right time.

The balance framework and the eight ways of thinking and being are valuable mental models—tools for the mind. They do not provide the answer. Instead, like the *Tao*, they are guides to ways of thinking that lead to better solutions, better strategies, and better execution. The framework is a structure and a guide that enables the leader to envision, grasp, and understand the leadership challenge at hand. The eight ways of thinking and being—what's inside the leader—inform, nurture, and activate the good judgment, intuition, and balance required to collaborate and lead.

A Reflection: Observations from Interviews with Leaders in Balance

As one moves to higher levels within an organization, the need to be intentional and deliberate about what one says and what one models with one's behavior and decisions increases. One's behavior demonstrates a preference for the way one leads and manages that differentiates one and one's organization. Building individual collaborative competencies and organizational capabilities is critical. Those who excel will take higher leadership positions. However, one can be smart, talented, and skilled, but not be a leader. One's ways of thinking may not be aligned with one's organization.

A leader must be highly self-aware, not a self-promoter. A self-promoter individual will be personally ambitious and see people as tools. This person lacks understanding of themselves and situations, which will limit her/his potential. She/he will spend energy on her/himself instead of the organization—that's hard to cure. Such a person may also have a lack of self-confidence.

In addition to self-awareness, balance and self-reflection are important. Although these may be seen as a weakness—as a passive personality trait—in fact, balance and self-reflection enhance self-confidence and result in a better understanding of one's self and situation. Although quick action may appear to be a sign of strength, reflection provides a solid foundation for action that draws upon good judgment, intuition, and experience.

Where do leaders learn to lead regardless of their business? Surprisingly, none say they learned this in college or in their MBA program. Some learned from reading and personal experience, particularly those who are serious students of leadership. Some learned from the service—the Army or the Marines. Some learned from other leaders, but many learned from a mentor or a boss—good and bad experiences.

How does this connect across generations—leaders of today preparing leaders for tomorrow? The Baby Boomers (born between 1946 and 1964)—the leaders of today—grew up within the structured and predictable stability of the hierarchy developing a loyalty to the organization and a feeling of safety within that structure. The Gen Ys (born between 1977 and 1990) experience no corporate commitment; therefore, they feel no corporate loyalty. They are on a constant search to develop personal career options.

What does this mean for the challenge of leadership in the twenty-first century? It means that today's leaders must help younger employees understand the connection between their own values and mission in life to the core values and mission of the organization. If Gen Ys see that there is alignment, they are more likely to forge a strong bond with an organization and stay longer than the usual 18 months that most employees from age 18 to 25 years stay.

To benefit from The Kucia Balance Framework and become a leader in balance, one must reflect, learn, grow, and change. As such, one must master a shift in ways of thinking and being—the essential human dimensions of this collaborative way of leading long-living organizations in this twenty-first-century global society.

Part II

What Does It All Mean—Taking It to the Next Level

Chapter 7

New Behaviors That Correlate to The Eight Ways of Thinking

In this chapter, we will offer suggestions for a new set of behaviors for today's leaders drawn from interviews with successful executives in resilient organizations such as Procter & Gamble, The Boeing Company, and Parker Hannifin. We will describe building a leader from the inside out allowing the authentic self to be intentionally present in situations, such as leading the organization through turbulence and change.

We will recap The Eight Ways of Thinking and discuss behavior correlates that we have observed in leaders in balance across the country.

Behaviors for Way of Thinking #1— Approaches Leadership as a Relationship

We believe that Bob McDonald, Procter & Gamble, embodies this way of thinking. In our interviews with him, he made these telling statements about leadership:

> Maybe part of building trust is connecting with people and understanding them as people not just as employees—to say, "I care about you"; "I care about your family"; "I care about your children." My belief is that I can teach anybody all the behaviors of leadership, but if they don't love the people they work with, those behaviors will come off as not authentic.

Bob provides an example of a colleague (Jim McNerney of The Boeing Company) who he refers to as an authentic leader:

> You feel very comfortable in his presence. To again demonstrate that leadership is storytelling, I remember when Jim was brand new on the board, and he came out to review the business I was responsible for at the time. This was—I don't know how many years ago—maybe 2002, and one of our long-time scientists, a relatively older fellow, just completely froze up. It was the first time he had ever done a presentation to a member of the board and so, for him, that was a big deal in his career, even though he may have been older than Jim. Certainly, he knew more about the subject matter than any of us. Jim noticed he froze up. There were three directors there—Jim was one, and there were two others. Jim had the sense that this guy froze up. He jumped up, ran over to the guy, and started massaging his shoulders and telling him, "just relax," even before the guy broke apart, because he could sense it. While it sounds soapy describing it to you, it was very, very natural, and the guy could continue. When I think of Jim, that's the way I think of his leadership. He's very aware; he's very authentic; and he really cares about people, and it comes through in every meeting you have with him.

A leader who approaches leadership as a relationship engages in what we call "active listening," which is a sign of respect toward others. How do you know if someone is actively listening to you? What behaviors are apparent? Here are a few of such behaviors:

- The other person is maintaining eye contact when you speak instead of looking at papers or looking around the room.
- The other person is giving cues that they are connecting with you by nodding their head or making statements such as, "I understand."
- The other person is asking questions at appropriate times—when you're finished talking is an appropriate time—not when they feel like interrupting.

- The other person paraphrases what you've said to make sure they truly got your message.

Bob Kohlhepp, from Cintas, summarizes the art of listening nicely: "You know, you show respect for people by listening. My father used to say to me, 'Bob, you have two ears and one mouth for a reason.'"

A leader who approaches leadership as a relationship is willing to put their personal ego aside and work with others to find ways to help the organization survive and thrive. As Bob Kohlhepp put it, "I could care less whether it's my idea. What I'm after is what's the best answer."

A leader who approaches leadership as a relationship focuses on building trust and respect so that people follow them based on that trust, rather than because of their position in the organization. Trust building is a process, of course, that takes place moment by moment, interaction by interaction. Behaviors that, over time, build trust in relationships include the following:

- Doing what one says you will do every time...no excuses
- Saying what one means, in a straightforward yet respectful manner
- Demonstrating that one trusts one's direct reports by delegating, providing resources, and letting people do their work
- Keeping confidences that people share with one and letting people know when information they share must be passed on for ethical and legal purposes
- Supporting others' good ideas even when they aren't initially popular
- Writing one's thoughts down clearly and without ambiguity in written communications and
- Asking for others' opinion even when one has the power to make decisions unilaterally

A leader who approaches leadership as a relationship often shares expectations with direct reports. Directives are clear and straightforward. People have an opportunity to ask questions if they don't understand. A leader builds in process checkpoints for long-term projects so that staff have opportunities to double-check their work and ask questions. This leader makes it easy for people to say, "I don't understand," or, "I don't think this will work and here's why." Linda Gravett sets the stage for this type of atmosphere in her company staff meetings. The conference table is round. She sits in the middle of her team during meetings. Small, yet intentional, behaviors like this can be powerful.

McNerney told the authors, "If I just rely on command and control, I will lose that authenticity and credibility that is so important in today's world. People aren't going to put up with, nor should they put up with, people who depend on hierarchy for decision making."

Harry Nieman believes in setting clear expectations around performance competencies and ethical principles and behaviors. He works with his executive team on a continuing basis to openly discuss and update the company's code of ethics. This is not just a dialogue; the code of ethics is shared with all employees throughout the world. Training classes are held to ensure that each person understands how these principles translate to their daily work. We have found that a code of ethics and organizing principles around behaviors and values provide clarity for employees, suppliers, and customers. People yearn for clarity.

McNerney also told us during an interview, "I think leadership has to have personal values associated with it. In other words, people have to feel not only that you're authentic and credible, but also the values you've got are ones that others want." John Pepper of Procter & Gamble echoed this sentiment when he suggested to us, "The camaraderie around fulfilling the mission is what makes you a community."

After synthesizing interviews of leaders across several organizations, we have come to the conclusion that most of them act in a way that focuses on building relationships that are augmented by changing structure. This approach will continue to be successful in the global society of the next decade.

Behaviors for Way of Thinking #2—
Understands the Leader
Embodies the Brand Promise

Behaviors that embody the brand promise are important to A. G. Lafley. He told us, "I've wondered whether leadership could be developed into a scholarly pursuit, and I think you can learn a lot from biography, but I do think you can learn a lot from how leaders behave in similar situations. You can observe what leaders do in different situations, but I don't know what to do with a checklist of behavior-type approaches because I honestly don't—I think much of my leadership is far more intuitive than it is planned. It's who I am and who I've become and who I am continuing to become." Lafley goes on to say, "I've never spent a minute on that kind of stuff. I've never been to a single Dale Carnegie course or anything like that. I do take the time to reflect on what I'm going to say and how I'm going to say it when I'm in a situation with a large audience and I have a half-an-hour opportunity or an-hour opportunity and I want to communicate a specific message or engage in a very specific learning."

Lafley's quote represents a way of thinking about leadership from the inside out. Intuition and "who I am and who I've become" is the source of his way of leading. He sees no value in a checklist of leadership behaviors. He wants to know how and when a leader would use certain behaviors, that is, the applicability.

Before a leader can embody their organization's brand promise, they must clearly understand that brand promise. In this context, we suggest that a brand could mean one of the following:

- The essence of who you are
- Features and attributes
- Performance and
- A set of values

Given this definition, a leader who wants to embody the brand promise of an ethical organization, for example, would engage in behavior, such as, driving out fear of retaliation for raising ethical issues; establishing and communicating ethical guidelines; consistently modeling the company's published values; and ensuring that core values are incorporated into strategic imperatives.

In an interview, Bob McDonald said,

> As leaders, we have to decide what we want our brands to stand for—what the equity of our brand is. When we think about branding, we think about the points of sameness and the points of difference. I always want at least a part of my equity to be about character, to be about putting the needs of the organization above myself, about always telling the truth, having integrity, not lying or cheating, not tolerating people who do, and about taking responsibility and being open to criticism. I try to model what we call the *Five E's* behaviors: *envision; engage; enable; energize;* and *execute.*

When we talked with people who know and work with Bob, they described him using similar terms. It's apparent that his branding efforts pay off!

Behaviors for Way of Thinking # 3— Motivated by a Higher Purpose; Mission Drives the Numbers

We turn again to those we interviewed to describe critical behaviors for this way of thinking. Michael J. Graham, S. J., Xavier University shared, "Our initial purpose as an institution is being joined to some larger civil or civic purpose which we fulfill specifically through our institutionally-distinct mission. That is to say, we will serve society not as a social-service center, not as a hospital, not as something other than a university. And so the contribution that we make to society needs to be made specifically as a university, and so the great trick is to realize that it is by being an excellent example of what you are that you will do the best job you can in terms of helping build up the work around you."

A. G. Lafley, Procter & Gamble, said,

> I don't know that I ever said "I don't believe in the vision thing" because I actually *do believe*, very strongly, in the purpose. One of the things that attracted me to the company in the beginning was that it was a company that believed in service, and it was a company that believed that its mission was to improve everyday lives, in a modest way, through the brands and the products and the services. It's a company that's very clear about whom we serve. I mean we're in business to make women and their families' lives a little bit better. So I think we're purpose-oriented.

McNerney believes that driving home the organizational mission across all levels is one of his primary roles. He said,

> I have to be very clear and articulate our mission in simple language. By the way, this is where I think our mutual friend, A. G. Lafley, is unsurpassed. A leader has to clarify "what we're going to do as an organization" and "what our strategy is." I work hard on this messaging. Then, the way I find out whether or not people are connecting with it is I go talk to them.

Behaviors for Way of Thinking #4—
Understands Collaboration Must
Have a Business Purpose

Don Washkewicz is very intentional about how and when he interacts with others at all levels within his company. He shared these thoughts with us during his interview:

> The key is, though, you have to be visible. So I think getting around like I had to do early on, and still do—of course it's tougher and tougher because we keep acquiring more businesses—and really interfacing with the people and meeting the people in the facilities, getting them to feel like they're part of the team and that they mean something. I go to the facilities

and I shake everybody's hand. I don't care if their hands are greasy or dripping with chips and oil, or whatever, I shake their hand because I mean that as "you're part of the team."

A leader who understands that collaboration must have a business purpose builds relationships within the organization with people who add to his or her strengths. The reality of limited time and energy results in the necessity for leaders to build alliances with others who add value to their own contributions because of skills or talents they have that the leader does not. An underlying premise is that the leader has the humility to recognize that he/she has shortfalls—not every CEO has the gift of computer savvy or hiring the right people for the right place and time, for instance. The CEO will need to seek out others within the organization that *do* have those talents, provide them with the resources to fill those voids and listen to their advice. Harry Nieman told us, "When building networks, it's important to go beyond the CEO's comfort zone of collaborating with people like himself/herself or with a similar background who are likely to become 'yes' people."

A leader who understands that collaboration must have a business purpose guides team efforts and meeting results to those that support the organization's mission. At Meridian Bioscience, CEO Jack Kraeutler asks that team charters throughout the organization have a purpose and objectives that are clearly aligned with Meridian's mission statement. When teams make recommendations to his executive team, Jack asks team members how each recommendation is aligned with the organization's mission. People have learned not to come to the executive team unless recommendations fulfill that requirement.

A leader who understands that collaboration must have a business purpose has an end result in mind when she/he calls meetings, makes appointments, picks up the telephone, or sends an email. Each request of someone to work together for a task, short- or long-term, involves moving toward the company's mission and vision. Each performance review a leader conducts has the mission and vision in the forefront.

Behaviors for Way of Thinking #5— Believes in Sharing Power and Spreading Leadership Authority

Tom Cody, former executive vice president at Macy's Inc., shared these thoughts with us:

> As I got older and had more experience, I realized two things. Number one, I'd never get home if I didn't learn how to delegate and rely on other people, and, secondarily, I think the fact of recognizing that the most important transition point was a willingness to recognize and articulate what I didn't know because once you do that and you know what you know and you know what you don't know, you're able to manage not only the tasks but define the objectives putting together the partnerships necessary. A way of augmenting and strengthening, really, the hierarchy is to import this and then that person—that person who knows when—has the good judgment experience and intuition to know when to pull the trigger in trying to make a decision, or how to encourage more learning to find the right answer.

John Lechleiter at Eli Lilly had this insight as he was preparing to step into the role of CEO in 2008. He thought to himself, "Don't get too carried away, Buster. Everybody's going to tell you what's on your shoulders. You need to realize you can't humanly do that yourself. You have to enable all of these other people to do it."

Marilyn Shazor at Southern Ohio Regional Transit Authority (SORTA) summarizes this thinking beautifully. She told us, "You're not always going to be the person who is leading. Sometimes you just really have to follow."

For many CEOs, one of the most-challenging aspects of sharing power is the development of leadership-continuity initiatives, also known as succession planning. Especially in family-owned businesses, it's difficult to admit that there will come a day when retirement is inevitable and people must be in place with the right stuff to take over the reins of leadership. At Macy's Inc., succession planning is a very intentional effort. Tom Cody stated in an interview,

> At every board meeting, we do an update to the board on succession-planning talent. It's a complete focus on what that next layer is—what the company would look like ten years from now under different structures to try to demonstrate to the board and to push us that leadership talent is in place subject to development, and that's a big deal for us.

At several of Gravett' s client organizations, CEOs have, with her assistance, developed specific, directed assignments for emerging leaders. These assignments are two pronged in purpose: provide development opportunities for young talent, and ensure that the organization has the skills, knowledge, and abilities to ensure growth and resiliency. Below are some examples of those directed assignments and the competencies they are designed to support.

Directed Assignments

Competency

Objective setting and results orientation to achieve strategic plans;

Assignments

- Benchmark and analyze strategic planning methods of three to five global organizations; present results to colleagues
- Facilitate the strategic planning session of another division within the organization
- Identify the processes and activities that provide competitors with an advantage
- Present results to colleagues

- Coach director-level and mid-manager-level staff through their strategic planning sessions
- Develop a written action plan to share lessons learned from organizational failures to managers and directors
- Join a task force to develop a performance management process that supports strategic plan execution
- Champion a continuous improvement recommendation or a process improvement team
- Do a problem prevention analysis
- Design new, simpler effectiveness measures

Reading List
- *The Balanced Scorecard*[1]
- *First, Break All the Rules*[2]
- *Creating a Culture of Competence*[3]

Behaviors for Way of Thinking #6—
Believes Teaching and Leadership
Have a Great Deal in Common

Bob Kohlhepp, Cintas, told us that he has encountered this type of leadership: "I read and I listen to writers such as Jim Collins but, I would say, without question, the greatest influence on me as a leader has been my boss, Dick Farmer. He's an incredibly capable leader and motivator and I learned far more from him than anybody else."

Kohlhepp's approach has evolved from what he learned from this role model:

> But I have a pretty good ability to look at a situation and hear all the facts and think "I've got it; we should do this." What I've got to do is keep that to myself a little longer, in cases where I'm dealing with subordinates, to try to teach the subordinate to reach the conclusion without me telling them the answer.

Another of Linda's client companies, Empower Media Marketing in Cincinnati, Ohio, has leaders who embody the tenets of this way of thinking that allows people to learn, grow, and trust by spending time listening and getting to know one another in an ad hoc collaborative community. As the company's offices were being built, the executive team specifically requested that the architects design huddle corners where employees could discuss questions and issues on an ad hoc basis. In several convenient corners on each floor, are tables that seat up to four people. As employees are chatting about assignments and brainstorming ideas in the hallways, they are encouraged to sit for a few minutes and capture their thoughts. In this way, passing thoughts are shared and discussed—they are not forgotten as people go back to their office and engage in other tasks. Anyone, at any level, can call a huddle and teach others what they know about a particular topic or customer need.

Leaders who believe that teaching and leading have a great deal in common learn from their mistakes and share what they have learned with others—embarrassing though that may be. Bob Kohlhepp was very frank in his interview with us about how he was a command-and-control type of leader early on in his career. He told us, as he's told others, that this was a mistake and has changed his way of thinking over time. Early in his career, people wanted to quit because of him. Today, he's a respected and emulated leader at Cintas.

Marla Phillips, former Merck quality control officer, benefited early in her career from leaders who believed that there is a correlation between leadership and teaching. In our interview, she said,

> They gave me that opportunity to kind of groom me for future positions knowing that I was green. But it was safe, and the plant manager there knew as much about quality as the rest of the quality people, so he wasn't trying to push product out the door to make money. Although he wasn't my direct boss, I really enjoyed working for him. I have the kind of personality where if I don't know something, I'll just come right out and say, "I have absolutely no idea what you're talking

about." We'd walk through it, and once we'd go through the scenario then I could apply what I learned to a bunch of different things.

Behaviors for Way of Thinking #7— Has a Personal Comfort with and Values Diversity

SORTA's, Marilyn Shazor said the following in response to a question about the effect of globalization, different cultures, and diverse languages on her company:

> Diversity brings creativity. The United States doesn't have it coined how to run public transportation. There are other countries that do it very well. We're a fairly decent-sized transportation organization and we don't have any Asians employees. I think it would add a lot to our organization and bring new ideas and concepts to the table. I'm all for globalization.

We have found that effective leadership for developing and leveraging a diverse workforce requires intentional behaviors to move the organization along this continuum (figure 7.1).

Leaders who promote the status quo make it clear that they are not interested in recruiting a diverse workforce. Instead, they look for employees and managers who look like and act like themselves. They do not express an interest in the potential growth that diverse perspectives and talents could bring to the company. Instead, they express satisfaction that people similar to themselves will accomplish the company's objectives.

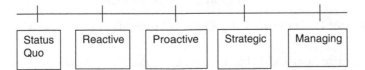

Figure 7.1   Stages along the diversity continuum.

Leaders in the reactive phase respond to court challenges or grievances from employees or candidates who believe they've been discriminated against based on age, race, or other demographic characteristics. The goal of these leaders is to minimize court costs or damage to their public image.

Proactive leaders start change efforts in their culture by taking steps, such as forming intentionally diverse teams and task forces, in order to promote innovation and minimize "group think." Their efforts may not be part of an overarching strategic effort, however, they do encourage employees to work effectively with people different from themselves and provide educational opportunities to ensure that these efforts are successful.

Strategic leaders make certain that inclusion and leveraging diversity are components of their company's strategic planning process. They seek out information about their customers—or potential customers—and determine the skills and talents that will be required in order to meet their needs. These leaders take steps to ensure that their employee population also mirrors their customers or constituents to demonstrate that the company wants to understand their needs.

Leaders who are managing diversity are making thoughtful, intentional efforts across the organization on a daily basis to make certain that 100 percent of their workforce is effectively utilized 100 percent of the time. They focus on ways to tap into every employee's talents, regardless of their age, race, or gender.

Behaviors for Way of Thinking #8—Believes the Challenge of Leading Change Is about Leadership in Balance not Control

Michael J. Graham, S. J., Xavier University, said recently,

> And so it is inevitable that making decisions comes with the call of leadership. And so it is incumbent upon the leader to

make decisions and that's probably one of the main things that a leader must do. Decision making can be collaborative, but not the act of making decisions itself. That rests with the leader. It's everything else about the decision making though that must be collaborative, I think. On the other end of the decision—on the front end—what collaboration is, by another name, is listening.

A. G. Lafley, Procter & Gamble, said,

I think a lot of leadership is situational. By situational, I mean effective leaders are self-aware and they are good at sizing up the situation, understanding what's needed, and then providing the leadership that's appropriate in that situation at that time. So, I think, in my time at P&G, I've tried to take on the leadership role that was required given the situation I was in. To be specific about the CEO situation three and a half years ago, the company was in a bit of a crisis, and it wasn't just a crisis of not delivering the results we committed to publicly and to our shareholders and to our employees and to ourselves; it wasn't about missing an earnings estimate; it wasn't about the stock price dropping in half or more; it was really, I think, much more about we'd lost our confidence and we'd lost our way. So what I tried to do was to help us find our way and, in doing so, restore our confidence. It wasn't anything more complicated than that.

Here, Lafley demonstrates the impact and influence on the leader's way of thinking—what he sees, how he understands and interprets its meaning for the organization—that gives rise to the strategy and ultimate actions taken.

One of Gravett's clients is the CEO of a high-tech organization in the Midwest. When he first took this position, he would attend departmental meetings with eagerness. He had lots of ideas about how to improve each department and he wanted to share them. Initially, he'd bring up a problem or deficiency in the department and let meeting participants know that he wanted to brainstorm ideas for solutions. Before he'd invite ideas, though, he'd offer his suggestions. He couldn't understand why no one made additional recommendations after he was finished sharing his thoughts.

Linda suggested to the CEO that he have the discussion topic placed on the agenda, invite solutions as before, but not make any of his own recommendations until after he had heard from everyone else at the meeting. She also suggested that he position himself at the center of the table rather than at the head of the table. The subtle message became, "Your ideas are important. I don't need to control the meeting." Once employees understood that the CEO truly wanted their input, the solutions flowed. The CEO has been participating in brainstorming meetings like this for two years now with a great deal of success.

In this chapter, we began to correlate new behaviors with The Eight Ways of Thinking and demonstrated The Kucia Balance Framework in action. We will continue this approach in chapter 8.

In chapter 9, we hear our leaders speak in their own voice and directly share the rich and deliberate balanced thought that undergirds and gives rise to their leadership actions. These excerpts offer insights into the challenges, the situations and thinking of successful skilled leaders in balance. We will ask you, the reader, to reflect on your own way of thinking and, using The Kucia Balance Framework as a guide, to tune into and get a feel for how these leaders think and balance the use of the *power* and *together* sides of the framework.

A Reflection

We are not mind readers; that's a talent neither of us can claim. So then, at a distance, we must look to how people behave in a variety of situations to intuit what they are thinking. If we have the opportunity, as we did in so many interviews, to have a face-to-face dialogue, we can simply ask, "What's your thought process when you take this step or that action?" We've shared those responses that we believe are the most telling—that demonstrate how one moves from thought to action in a meaningful way—the ways of thinking that give rise to the behaviors of leaders in balance.

Chapter 8

The Kucia Balance
Framework in Action

In this chapter, we'll continue with a more concrete discussion about how leaders are thinking as they navigate the often-complex global workplace, utilizing elements of The Kucia Balance Framework. We'll share how CEOs we interviewed use this framework and recommend ways that the reader can effectively operate within this approach.

To help refresh your recollection of The Kucia Balance Framework, review chapter 4 where we introduce and fully develop the culture, the structure, the leadership, the change, and the challenge for the *power* and *together* sides of the framework.

Here's a positive example of using the *power* side of the framework. Gravett was in the hospital a couple of years ago for major surgery. As she was going under the anesthetic, she was calmed by the knowledge that her surgeon was an assertive, skilled person who was likely to act quickly in the event of an emergency. If immediate action were to be required, she could not imagine the surgeon taking time to bring the surgery team to consensus. The doctor would simply take appropriate action based on his knowledge, experience, and expertise.

There are times when CEOs must operate in much the same way. Key questions the CEO should be addressing are as follows:

- Is there a time constraint within which this issue must be addressed—not an artificial time constraint, but a true deadline?

- Is there a quality requirement that means one solution is likely to be the most rational over several potential solutions (e.g., safety considerations)?
- Do I have enough information to make a high-quality decision?
- Is the problem structured (i.e., budget, resources, time frame, regulatory guidelines)?
- If I make the decision myself, am I reasonably certain that stakeholders will accept the decision?

In our interview with Bob McDonald, he provided an excellent insight into choosing between the option of making decisions unilaterally or through consensus. He suggested the following analogy to a living organism when referring to his company:

> When you've got 138,000 people constantly pushing the boundaries of this organism and in a world that's constantly changing, that's volatile, uncertain, complex, and ambiguous, aren't you better off having 138,000 people trying to figure out the direction to go versus one person do that?

We agree. One person cannot be the sole source of knowledge in today's complex organizations. John Lechleiter told us he was much calmer about taking the helm once he realized that he could not know everything and should not *try* to reach that impossible goal.

There may be occasions when a CEO wishes to mentor or coach a direct or indirect report so that the person is clear on the organization's culture, stakeholders, marketplace, competition, or all of the above. In this type of situation, the mentee must understand and appreciate the expertise of the leader as well as the value of the guidelines and recommendations they are providing. There are those times when mentees, because of their lack of experience or expertise, must actively listen. Their experience may not be sufficient in some areas for them to offer tested solutions. Their most important role is that of student. The mentor will operate on the power side of the framework in this type of scenario.

Any leader, regardless of experience or expertise, is likely to be challenged by people within their organization at one time or another. This is especially likely today considering the large number of Gen X and Gen Y employees who don't automatically assign respect and authority to leaders who happen to have CEO after their name. During these potentially tense occasions, a CEO might have to take back authority in order to present a united front to customers or groups of employees or shareholders.

Gravett was having dinner with a client who was entertaining potential customers from out of the country. That evening, two computer technicians were also included because they could address very specific technical questions the potential customers might ask. At one point, the question was, "Is it possible to have a prototype available within a one-month time frame?" The two technicians immediately answered, "No, this is not possible because of our busy schedules." The CEO had to immediately interject with the assertion that, "yes, the company could make the prototype available within the requested time frame." He was the sole person at the table who could make the decision to hire extra staff or subcontractors to ensure this type of deadline could be met. His statement made an unequivocal point to the customers and the technicians: he was in charge.

Gravett has another client that is a small manufacturer in the Midwest. During an employee meeting she attended one evening, a group of managers was complaining that the human resources manager made them follow policies such as FMLA (Family and Medical Leave Act) and ADA (Americans with Disabilities Act). The managers complained that these "policies" established by the human resources manager were time consuming and cumbersome to follow and they asked the

CEO to override "her" policies. The CEO took this opportunity to explain that the human resources manager didn't write the laws; she was responsible for ensuring that their company was in compliance with the laws. He also took the opportunity to explain that lawsuits from people who were aggrieved by a company's failure to comply with laws of this nature could bankrupt a company. He then asked how many people wanted to be out of a job because their company went bankrupt after paying out damages for an employee claim. No one raised their hand, so he quickly moved on to the next question.

In situations with seasoned employees that appear appropriate for moving to the *together* side of the framework for coaching purposes, the leader should be asking questions such as the following:

• Does there appear to be a skills deficiency that is holding this person back?
• Does the person seem motivated to provide quality work?
• Does the person understand how to access and use available resources?

John Lechleiter had this to say about coaching others who are past the ingenue stage:

> When I hear people moaning and complaining about how this isn't going to work and that isn't going to work, I tend to say, "Well, I may not have the solution, but clearly, you have the problem." And most people accept that; most people don't want you to solve their problems for them.

There are situations in which leaders who want to move to the *together* side of the framework use technology as a means to foster networking. In today's high-tech, low-touch business environment, efficiency rules supreme—sometimes at the cost of rich, face-to-face communication. The Communications Model

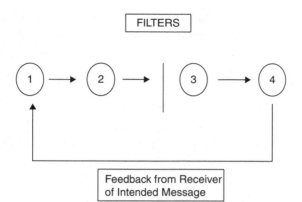

Figure 8.1   Communications Model. Copyright © Gravett and Associates, 1998.

that Gravett developed in figure 8.1 depicts how filters, such as email or video conferencing, can provide a barrier between the message intended and the message received. The objective behind moving to the *together* side of the framework cannot be achieved if filters like these aren't minimized (figure 8.1). Filters are any dimension of diversity such as age or gender.

When filters such as inappropriate email use exist, the leader must be especially careful to be crystal clear about intent, frames of reference, and decision-making accountability. The leader isn't able to see a quizzical look in the email reader's eyes or a frustrated shrug of the shoulders. For this reason, we recommend a high level of face time when you are attempting to build rapport and understanding.

There are clearly times when employees, customers, or vendors do not respond to the autocratic approach. As a matter of fact, rather than complying with a leader's dictates without the opportunity for input, many people in today's workplace will simply vote with their feet and leave in search of a more open workplace. Leaders should operate on the *together* side of the framework whenever feasible to minimize the chances of this occurring in their organization.

Bob Kohlhepp had a succinct way of making an excellent point about communication during his interview. He said,

You're supposed to listen twice as much as you talk. You've got to understand the human tendency when you're discussing something with somebody. Listen to what they're saying; try to understand their perspective and where they're coming from. It's a whole lot easier to disagree with somebody if they think you give a damn about what they think.

Gravett was asked by a client to facilitate an employee meeting for a 120-employee Southern organization. The mandate of the CEO was clear: the meeting objective was to surface ideas from all employee levels about how to expand services and products to existing customers and attract new customers. No idea was to be dismissed, at least until there was an opportunity to explore the idea over time. As Gravett was prepping the CEO for his role in the employee meeting, she suggested that he participate as a team member in the brainstorming breakout sessions. At first, he thought that meant that he should lead the dialogue and have all the best ideas. She had to elaborate on the notion of "team member." This meant that he would sit at the round conference table with other employees and offer ideas alongside them. Some of the other ideas offered might be more actionable than his. He was relieved that he didn't have the pressure of coming up with the "best" ideas. The CEO took this approach and successfully blended into the groups he joined without overshadowing any one individual. To reiterate what Bob Kohlhepp said to us, "Who cares who's right as long as we come up with the right idea."

Bob McDonald holds similar views on what he calls his company's "democracy of ideas." He told us,

My challenge whenever I teach is how do I make sure I draw out the individuals and let them teach each other—learn from each other—because sometimes that's more valuable than me pontificating. Oftentimes somebody's judgment will persuade me differently on a particular issue.

In another of Gravett's client companies, Car-Part.com, CEO Jeff Schroder is one of the company founders and has a product development background. He's tempted every single day to veer off his strategic path into the weeds and micromanage product developers. He waits for their input on projects before making decisions from his thirty-thousand-foot perspective. He must rely on their input because there are hundreds of small decisions they are making hour by hour to ensure product viability that he cannot, and should not, keep up with. What he does encourage, however, is the continuous communication cross-functionally that's necessary to understand customer needs, manufacturing issues, and distribution challenges. He also encourages close, informal working relationships that foster behind-the-scenes resolution of small problems before they become serious enough to warrant his attention. Besides, Jeff has repeatedly said that he believes individuals throughout the company must feel responsible for the success of projects they're involved with. Employees must act like owners.

Interacting on a frequent basis with employees is another activity on the *together* side. Sometimes employees want to get to know their CEO on a personal level. We believe it's important to allow this to happen in an appropriate way. We found that Jim McNerney agrees with this approach as well. During our interview, he said,

> I spend a fair amount of time with employees. If I've done a good job of creating an environment that encourages open feedback, I'll get that feedback. I spend a lot of time at the Boeing Leadership Center, which is where I meet thousands of employees. I have to stay open and stay connected.

Employee surveys and focus groups are designed to capture peoples' candid opinions and ideas about the leadership and culture of an organization. In many cases, employees aren't completely open because they believe retribution will be forthcoming as a result of their honesty. Yet CEOs need to know that new ideas and products will truly work, and who knows better than the people doing the work whether ideas are implementable? The CEO who wants to surface employees' honest opinions will find more success operating on the *together* side of the framework.

Michael J. Graham, S. J. of Xavier, describes his leadership style as a very personal way of being:

> My desire to listen before making a decision is based on my own personal way I'm put together. I like to make people feel included more than excluded at my best. And so bringing people into decision making and so on through active listening is an important part of that. But also, I have come to believe that there are all kinds of gifts and skills and abilities and visions out there and not to sample them broadly. Tap them well, before you plunge off in a direction that would be to render a decision more defective, or not as strong. That also bridges to the other side of the moment of decision, because there is nothing worthwhile to do in life that a person can accomplish alone, I think really. The most important things to be done are things that can only be accomplished together. To the degree to which people have a sense of ownership at stake, participation, or whatever in the decision-making process up front helps to pave the way for their own active participation afterwards as well.

We want to reiterate that team efforts, or collaboration, are not appropriate in every circumstance. If this approach is forced on a situation that doesn't fit, negative outcomes will surely follow. Gravett has consulted with organizations in which an autocratic leader went to a seminar about participative management and decided that he wanted to adopt this approach throughout his organization. The mandate came down: "There will be teams and teambuilding activities, starting immediately." Unless there is a context and guidelines or structure this does not work. Too often, a leader will use elastic authority, giving authority to start teams and just as quickly snap back control when the team moves in a direction he does not like. Mandating a culture change is not the same as moving through the P-A-C-E of change described in chapter 3, where there is a context and a purpose behind collaboration.

You might recall from chapter 3 that the PACE-of-change concept takes people through four stages of change: preparation; acceptance; commitment; and execution. We can incorporate the PACE model into The Kucia Balance Framework for discussion about which steps in the process fall onto the power side and which fall onto the *together* side (figure 8.2).

During the preparation, building acceptance, and building commitment phases of implementing change, a leader takes many unilateral steps. However, there comes a point at which the leader must empower employees and peers to take their own steps, in their own segments of the workplace, to execute change. If the leader forces them into the execution phase too strongly, the effectiveness of the approach drops off dramatically. To sustain change, there needs to be an intentional time to pass the torch to employees so that changes in behavior actually occur and momentum doesn't fall off.

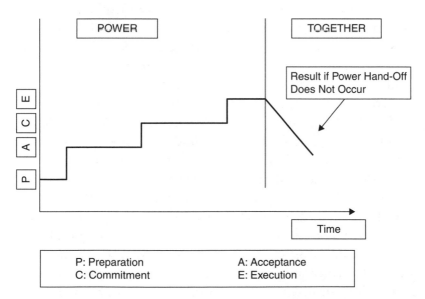

Figure 8.2 The PACE of change and leadership in balance.

There are times when a leader must cross from one side of the framework to the other within a very short time frame—as short as one day in some cases. For instance, a collaborative leader may find that no one else has specific expertise to make a decision other than themselves and there is no time to develop the expertise in others because the decision must be made immediately. To minimize this dilemma from becoming a frequent occurrence, leaders can follow Bob Castellini's approach about getting the right people in the right place at the right time. He said that his primary focus with The Cincinnati Reds is putting people into the right positions, both in the offices and on the field. In his words, "You can't do anything without competent people around you."

Sometimes circumstances compel an autocratic leader to move toward collaboration, even if he is accustomed to making unilateral decisions. One of Gravett's client companies went through a streamlining process over the course of a year, resulting in a much flatter structure. The CEO previously could explain his power guarding by saying that "he couldn't possibly arrive at consensus with the large leadership team across the organization." When the company was acquired and left with a flat structure, after the dust settled the leadership team was much smaller. There was nowhere to hide. The CEO was forced to call on his leadership team more often and actually found that spreading the decision making caused him to feel less stress. Being at the top suddenly became less lonely.

Tom Cody, former executive vice president of Macy's, shared a similar experience from his early leadership years. He said that before he came to Macy's he was in the airline business. He was given a great deal of responsibility early on, without much training to build his leadership competencies. At that time, he said he tended to be much more controlling, partly because of his inexperience and partly because of lack of confidence. This resulted in his reluctance to put success in somebody else's hands. However, as the years went by and he gained more experience, Tom realized that he spent all of his waking hours at the office and wouldn't ever have a home life if he didn't start relying on other people. Most importantly, Tom told us that he realized he needed to recognize and articulate what he didn't know so he could build the partnerships necessary for his and the organization's success. He believes that his life became so much easier when he came to this realization.

Chapter 9

Learning from Mentors through The Eight Ways of Thinking

Through these candid excerpts, we are privileged to listen and to learn from a talented group of successful executives who are more humble than heroic; who develop relationships and personal influence as the foundation for their leadership; who set the tone by living the values of their organization; who encourage collaboration by spreading leadership, authority, and responsibility with a clear and accountable purpose—to make better decisions and to execute them better; who take seriously the role of leader as a teacher and a learner; who clearly understand the challenge of globalization and the value of diversity of people and ideas; and finally, although they value collaboration, they are comfortable making hard decisions because they trust their own good judgment, instincts, and intuition.

Don Washkewicz shared with us,

> I would say I really had the advantage of having several really good mentors. We didn't talk about them being mentors in the sense that, hey, I'm going to mentor you and I'm going to spend a lot of time with you. I worked very closely with both of those fellows throughout my career and was in many, many meetings with them. What I learned from just watching them, watching them work, watching them handle different situations was tremendous, so I really had the benefit of some very good role models.

In this chapter, we have created a mentoring-like opportunity for you to raise your awareness, your ability to recognize and to become more familiar with The Eight Ways of Thinking and The Kucia Balance Framework by listening closely and reflecting on the thoughts of some skilled leaders in balance.

Collaborative leadership in balance begins with a shift in ways of thinking that was evident throughout the conversations we conducted with our research participants. The following are select excerpts from those conversations that illustrate the deeper dimensions of their thinking across The Eight Ways of Thinking.

Instead of paraphrasing and synthesizing their thoughts, we are allowing these leaders to speak in their own voice and directly share the rich, deliberate, and balanced thought that undergirds and precedes their leadership actions. These are more than quotes or sound bites from a transcript; these excerpts offer insights into the challenges, the situations, and the thinking of successful and skilled leaders in balance, thus creating a unique opportunity to learn from this talented and successful group of mentors.

For you, the reader, this is an exercise in critical thinking and critical listening, both essential skills for leaders in balance. As you read through each of these excerpts, we ask you to: (1) reflect on your own way of thinking, (2) use The Kucia Balance Framework to tune into/get a feel for how these leaders balance the use of the *power* and *together* sides of the framework, and (3) ponder how these ways of thinking inform and influence the *head of a strategist, a moral and ethical heart*, and the *hand of a collaborative leader in balance.*

The following figure depicts the interrelationship between The Eight Ways of Thinking and the *head, heart,* and *hand* of a leader of a long-living organization in the twenty-first-century global society (figure 9.1).

To assist you in this personal reflection, we have organized these excerpts by The Eight Ways of Thinking and we have highlighted some mentoring thoughts that will help you

	Head (I) (Strategy)	Heart (II) (Culture)	Hand (III) (Leadership)
The Ways of Thinking of a Leader in Balance: A Brand of Collaborative Leader of a Living Organization	Critical Thinker Reflective Strategist	Moral-Ethical Builder of Trust	Collaborative Shares Power + Authority Encourages Innovation
1. Approaches leadership as a relationship not a position			■
2. Understands that the leader embodies the brand promise		■	
3. Is motivated by a higher purpose and believes that mission drives the numbers	■		
4. Understands that collaboration must have a business purpose	■		
5. Thinks "outside of the pyramid" in order to share power and spreads leadership authority and responsibility			■
6. Believes teaching and leadership have a great deal in common		■	■
7. Understands that at the center of collaboration is a personal comfort with and valuing of diversity	■	■	
8. Believes that the challenge of leading change is about leadership in balance not control	■	■	

I. A person, a master teacher and master learner, who thinks critically and reflectively with the Head of a Strategist, able to lead an organization that has the ability to learn (sensitive to the environment) and govern its own growth and evolution (wise financing and use of resources)

II. A person who nurtures the heart and soul of the organization and its individuals and makes choices and decisions with a Moral and Ethical Heart, able to lead an organization that has the ability to build community and a persona for itself (cohesion and identity)

III. A person who first chooses to serve others through a higher purpose and executes strategy with the Hand of a Collaborative Leader, able to lead an organization that has the ability to build constructive relationships with other entities within and outside (tolerance and decentralization)

Figure 9.1 Leader in balance. Copyright © Kucia-Gravett, 2008.

identify both The Eight Ways of Thinking and The Kucia Balance Framework in action. For many of the excerpts, we have also indicated which side of The Kucia Balance Framework, *together* (T) or *power* (P), is influencing the mentoring thought.

Identifying Both The Eight Ways of Thinking and The Kucia Balance Framework in Action

Approaches Leadership as a Relationship not a Position

This leader shows respect for people by listening closely; creates bonds of friendship, camaraderie, and loyalty to the institution; engenders a sense of humility balanced with enormous organizational ego; and shares power and authority. This way of thinking influences the hand—the way a leader goes about building relationships motivated by a higher purpose. You will notice that most of the excerpts reflect the *together* (T) side of the balance framework.

John Lechleiter offers this candid thought: "The more I read about leadership, the less I feel that I know. You think you've got the genie in the bottle at some point in your life and then, as you go on, you realize that you've got so much more to learn [T]."

Don Washkewicz shared with us his honest first thoughts as he was named the CEO of Parker Hannifin, a $10 billion company:

First of all, I was amazed I even got this job to begin with because the CEO really was only asking me if I'd be interested. I almost died, I think, when he came out and told me. We toasted and he said, "Well, you're in." I said, "What do you mean I'm in?" He said, "Well, you got the job." I said, "What job?" He said, "They just voted you in." I said, "Oh my God!"

You know you do have to grow into that kind of thing, overtime, but all that comes down to is really—and I know you've heard it a thousand times—having the right people in the right jobs and so forth. If you say what else is critical here, you realize early on you can't do this yourself [T]. If you wanted to be Jack Welch and that kind of a leader, well, he's got his own certain kind of persona in that job. I would much rather get the mission real clear—out to the troops—have the best people in those jobs and let them take it forward [T]. Let them use their own creativity in getting things done instead of just trying to do it all myself. Everybody has a different style; that just happens to be my style.

Bob Kohlhepp of Cintas Corporation shares,

The reason sometimes I'm a hard-nosed son-of-a-buck is I'm trying to make you better. It's not because I like being a hard-nosed son-of-a-buck; it's because I'm trying to make you better. But it takes a while for a relationship to develop before people truly believe that, so to me that's gaining respect [T]. It's the relationship; it's good communication; a lot of discussion, and so forth. So, to me, that's why people follow somebody. So I think if you truly have people's best interests at heart, and you're trying to make somebody better, and you're trying to have the collective results of the whole organization, you've got to care about people to be a good leader. If you don't care about people, you will not be a good leader. You're going to be missing something—probably on the *together* side of the balance framework [T].

Bob McDonald offers an important caution about the leader who is more interested in her/his own success first:

Yeah, my belief is I can teach anybody all the behaviors of leadership, but if they don't love the people they work with, those behaviors will come off as not authentic [T]. In business it's difficult because you get—I don't want to characterize any one person, but you get people in who are personally ambitious and it's just not going to happen. If their ambition is for themselves rather than the organization, they're going to see the people as tools [P], and they're not going to get their kicks out of helping develop and grow those people. So I think this is true, but it's got to start with your own heart.

Understands That the Leader Embodies the Brand Promise

This leader is both noble and humble and, as such, embodies the values and principles of the organization; sets the tone by what is done and valued; understands that trust is the essential foundation for collaboration balanced with normal instincts for competition; addresses issues with honesty, integrity, respect, and affection for the dignity of others; models and communicates a set of expectations and preferences for behavior of other leaders throughout the organization. This way of thinking influences the heart of a moral and ethical leader. Each of these excerpts provides an encouraging insight of people who are in touch with the enormity of their task and yet grounded as leaders.

Jim McNerney begins with the simple statement,

> Leaders have to live our values [T+P], and that gets down to some personal, ethical, integrity kinds of definitions, and leaders have to deliver results. My mantra around here is that "as our people grow, our company grows." People who are excited about their personal growth are going to grow a company [T], and the way to get people excited about their personal growth is not only to teach them, but to help them. People have to feel not only that you're authentic and credible, but the values you've got are ones that others want, too [T]. I think good leaders have to be reasonably facile, smart enough to be able to solve problems, and work with people to solve problems. In good leaders, I see an element of courage that they've got in the sense of making difficult decisions, facing into tough people problems and that, oftentimes, takes some element of courage [T+P].

Bob McDonald believes, "The minute you have to rely on your authority to get something done, you've lost. The way I exercise my authority is by building trust. I build trust; I try to build trust with everyone that I work with [T]. I try every day to build so much trust that if, when I need to, I can withdraw money from that emotional bank account without the risk [P] of the person believing that I'm not on their team and I'm not on their side." McDonald rarely resorts to the use of his power and authority to get something done.

McDonald makes the observation,

> I think the best leaders are highly self-aware and that, to me, is kind of like a common denominator. Those leaders who struggle lack self-awareness. Some even good leaders lack self-confidence, and some even go as far as to be self-promoters, and I think that gets in the way of being a really good leader because if you're busy self-promoting, it's hard for you to get in touch with reality [P+T]. I do think reflection and balance are important even in this issue because what you're describing could be construed to be—they aren't, but they could be—construed to be passive personality traits, and that has a somewhat negative connotation to it [T+P]. What they do is actually enhance self-confidence, and it's counterintuitive [T+P].

Marla Phillips talked about how she handles an employee who has made a mistake and what she learned from observing the employees' reaction:

> Basically, I say own up to it, and we'd own up to it together. So there's no one model other than a pretty calm approach [T]. Once he saw how I responded—I actually saw it on his face. Apparently, the traditional management styles have made people very nervous about owning up to mistakes. They were hammered if they did [P].

"Notice I didn't say that the leader must be smarter than everybody else [T+P]," offered John Lechleiter. "A leader should be good at enabling and engaging other people's intellects, but a leader doesn't have to be the smartest person. That realization is actually quite liberating [T+P]. It hit me on the day when I was named CEO. I was walking to work, knowing that thirty minutes later the world was going to find out that I'm the next CEO of Lilly. On the one hand, I felt the weight of it all, but, on the other hand, I realized in a profound way that it really wasn't all up to me; there were 40,000 other smart people at Lilly who were going to take their piece of the load [T+P]."

John Pepper said, "Listening, really—caring about other people's individual—everybody counts—really matters to me. Not out of some simple moral precept, although I think there is a morality aspect to it, but I've just seen it so powerfully effective." But Pepper offered the following sage observation, "Arriving at your own belief and understanding, it's a priceless, priceless attribute that you don't see in that many people and you search for it always. Nobody does it perfectly, but it really is very special [T+P]."

Is Motivated by a Higher Purpose, a Mission, and Believes That Mission Drives the Numbers

This leader focuses attention on purpose, mission, and values of the institution to raise people's motivation above personal interest to service to society; realizes that sole focus on the bottom line may lead to short-term thinking not long-term life; understands that interdependence and collaboration are essential to accomplish the purpose and mission in any organization; and believes we must energetically collaborate on the inside so we can successfully compete on the outside.

Jim McNerney asks and answers the question,

> So how do I know people are aligned with our mission? I have to be very clear and articulate our mission in simple language. Then, the way I find out whether or not people are connecting with it is, I go talk to them. I spend a fair amount of time with employees. If I've done a good job of creating an environment that encourages open feedback, I'll get that feedback. It's a good sign that people are listening and thinking. I just have to stay open to the feedback and people have to know I'm open to it [T+P]. So I spend a lot of time at the Boeing Leadership Center, which is where I meet thousands of employees. I have to stay open and stay connected [T].

Bob Kohlhepp talks about mission as part of an organization's culture:

> Every organization has a culture; very few organizations take the time to define it; we have defined it. It's made up of our principle objectives which is our mission statement—what we call our company character—which is a group of adjectives and phrases that describe what we believe in, how we expect our people to conduct themselves [T+P] and so forth, and then our management system, which is how we have organized and manage the company.

Understands That Collaboration Must Have a Business Purpose

This leader is a pragmatist who believes you can't get good results if you can't collaborate; has gained personal maturity and new insights through successful experiences and results with collaboration; believes that collaboration, cooperation, and interdependence are a business and cultural necessity; knows that collaboration is harder than command and control requiring courage, commitment, and, sometimes, conflict as disagreement to differentiate the nature of a problem or solution; and understands the two parts of purpose driven collaboration as a means to an end: (1) to reach better decisions and strategies (to prepare for change) and (2) to execute the strategies better.

John Pepper begins by stating a clear purpose for collaboration: "I view collaboration as a means to get to the bottom-line results that we want. I don't view them as competing portions, but, rather, I view collaboration as I think you do—complementary to getting to the bottom-line [T+P]."

Richard Antoine, former global human resource officer at Procter & Gamble, talks about business as a team sport:

> If you aren't a good team player, if you don't collaborate well, you cannot be successful. So we'll have brilliant engineers, scientists, designers and marketers, whatever, but they aren't going to be running the company because we need people who can

collaborate with each other, and so it's a critical—absolutely critical skill. Collaboration to us extends beyond working well together. You've got to be able to work together with the various groups in the company, so that means being able to work across cultures, across sectors, across race, across all groups, and collaboration is a word we use a lot [T+P].

Jim McNerney thinks a lot about relationship building and collaboration—both with a purpose, though.

We're a business enterprise that produces results, so collaboration, to me, means getting the best out of teams beyond your own to produce the best results for the company [T+P]. Collaboration is a term I prefer because it implies that there has to be a business result, that someone is accountable for that result, and that a team is going to go get it [P]. Building relationships beyond your own team is important. In a business enterprise, relationships are important—trust is important—so that people will be willing to get into foxholes with each other. Ultimately, you'll end up having stronger relationships with people you have pushed and who have grown because you pushed them and because you've inspired them to reach higher. But you can't fall prey to "relationships for relationships' sake." It's not in the company's best interest—and it doesn't necessarily make people successful [T+P].

John Lechleiter wants the process of getting to a decision to be collaborative, "but increasingly, as I've developed as an executive, I try to be very clear about which individual is making the decision [T+P]. Nobody can tell me that 'a committee made a decision' and get away with it."

Thinks Outside of the Pyramid in Order to Share Power and Spread Leadership, Authority, and Responsibility throughout the Organization

This leader balances the present reality moving forward toward the future with an eye on the future shape and structure of the organization; envisions a new structure—an internal network of creative people collaborating on complex issues that require learning, entrepreneurial, creative, and innovative action—a network of influence, power, and learning that augments the hierarchy and is fluid in the situation. They have the skill and judgment (intuition and instinct) to know how and when to unify and orchestrate the network with the hierarchy.

John Lechleiter strongly believes,

> We need to make the world our playground as opposed to just the walls of our labs or our offices. That's a very different approach than the one that prevailed when I joined the company, and the skills required to do that on the part of our leaders are different [T+P]. Working with partners is hard as well. In fact, sometimes it can seem a lot harder than just doing everything ourselves. So, we've got to work on the new set of skills required to be good collaborators. It requires a different sort of leadership [T+P].

Lechleiter continues,

> With regard to our own people, there are three things. First, leaders need to focus on employee engagement. We have some of the smartest employees in the world and yet only get about ten percent of what a lot of them have to offer us. The problem is mainly with management; it's not our employees [T+P]. The second thing is teamwork, a good old-fashioned word that in a business such as ours, is essential. We need to get people out of their silos [T]. The third piece is getting to action—having the courage to act and to take risks, the willingness to accept that not everything is going to work, and a level of comfort with the fact that perfection is not required in every situation [T+P]. We are very analytical in our company and we're perfectionists. That's the culture and, in some respects, it's very good. But some points along this corporate DNA strand need to change. I want to give people permission to make the changes that are necessary [T+P].

McDonald observed,

> Well, for me the leadership model we use here at P&G is the one
> that I like the best, which is the *Five E's*—Envision, Engage,
> Energize, Enable, and Execute. As you and I have talked before,
> originally that was a *Three E* model, and we added Engage to
> reflect the importance of collaboration, particularly in this
> global, multi-cultural world, and also in our organization
> structure, which tends to be a segmented structure—a matrix
> structure—which requires collaboration, and then Execute.
> And Execute was added pretty much because of our culture
> [T+P]. Our culture in this company is we all want to be strate-
> gists; none of us wants to execute. You ask how many people
> work on execution and nobody raises their hand, yet we all work
> on execution. Of course, the only strategy the marketplace sees
> is the one we execute, so that's why we added Execute.

Washkewicz believes,

> Spread of influence and power—that's the name of the game
> around here. So that's the underpinnings of the whole thing;
> that's the most important part of the whole strategy. I need to
> empower employees to take this and execute on it [T]. Well, I
> think at all the levels we're collaborating, certainly at the senior
> level now working on everything that's going on here, I mean
> this requires collaboration across pretty much all the levels [T].

Marla Phillips observed,

> Looking at the balance framework I see two very different lead-
> ership styles, and this one, the *power* side, I saw a lot of evidence
> of young managers working hard more to please their bosses
> than trying to manage their groups. They were conditioned to
> know that they had to be able to instantly and correctly answer
> any random question their boss asked. So they spent hours put-
> ting together beautiful charts and metrics that would show their
> boss how productive their group was. It was all hierarchy [P].
> The *together* side of The Kucia Balance Framework is you really

understand what's going on, and you really understand the mission, and you really want to move the group towards something better. It can be irrespective of bosses. It's more stretching people's brains to think more [T].

Believes Teaching and Leadership Have a Great Deal in Common

This leader is both a teacher and a leader (1) who asks hard questions to stimulate learning in search of reality and truth; (2) who sets the right course and creates the right strategy in a disciplined, deliberate, and intentional manner; (3) who knows a master teacher must be a master learner who listens, is observant and curious; (4) who admits not having all the answers; (5) who is open to learning and somewhat vulnerable; and (6) who encourages learning through coaching.

John Lechleiter knows that, "people at Lilly hate to be told how to do something. They want to be given a challenge and some broad parameters and then left to their own devices. But there are times when a leader can get involved constructively [T+P]."

Lechleiter tells the story of a team at Lilly that had been tasked with completing an enormous regulatory submission by the end of the year.

We had made that goal public to our investors. Right before Christmas, I got a message from a high-ranking executive, saying, "John, somebody has to tell you that this is impossible to do and I want to walk you through the reasons why." Now, five or ten years ago, I would have said, "Tell me more. Let's have a meeting. Take me through it. I understand. Do the best that you can." But this time, my answer was different. I said, "Look, I appreciate all of the information and I see that it's a really tough challenge. But you guys know that you have access to any resource in the company. So, once we have everybody in the company working on this—including Christmas Day—if you still can't get this done by the end of the year, then come back to me and let me know. Otherwise, please get it done by December 31 as we agreed." They were done by December 24!

John Pepper firmly believes, "Teaching at its heart is about help-ing another person be all they can be [T]." He goes on to say,

> It involves reinforcing their strengths, elevating their expecta-tions, conveying trust in them [T]. They believe in people; they have lots of different styles. I always hate to talk about the word "style." Your style may be tough, gruff, softer, but they believe in the growth of people as a principle foundation for success and a principle expression of their reason that they exist [T]. Others have great values—integrity, pursuing truth wherever it leads, being realistic—a penchant to continue to learn and grow. It's a terribly important characteristic.

Pepper said in an interview, "Teaching in the sense of helping another person be all they can be involves a number of different things—expectations, trust, confidence." Thomas Friedman once said, "There is an enormous difference between a person who is critiquing you and they're doing it with the idea that they want you to be better [T], and another person is doing it because they're going to be telling you that you're not doing well [P]." Pepper continued, "You can smell the difference in a minute. You'll listen to the person who is really trying to help you and take in what they have to say no matter what it is. If you start to think you're being assaulted—it's the mindset with which one teaches."

Richard Farmer, former chairman and CEO of Cintas shared that one of his greatest points of pride in his career was not making a lot of money or doing $4 billion in business. Instead he said, "It's looking around this organization and saying, 'I remember when that guy came out of college and he was brash and he was awkward and look at him now [T].' So, yeah, that's where I get my biggest kick out of business is developing people. I can look around these halls and look at people; I can remem-ber them when they were just young sales people or something. All of a sudden they're running big chunks of our company."

Bob Kohlhepp says of his boss and mentor,

I would say without question, the greatest influence on me as a leader has been my boss, Dick Farmer. He's an incredibly capable leader and motivator, and I learned far more from him than anybody else. He was my mentor and still is. Well, yeah. I would say when I joined Cintas, I had my MBA; I was finishing my MBA. I was a CPA, and I don't know how smart I am, but I was smarter than the average bear. Dick saw in me somebody who was smart and somebody who had incredible will and determination, but everybody hated my guts. He said this is worth investing my time and effort to get this guy to figure this out, and it took him about a year or two. He was tough on me; he was tough. He is no powder puff. "I'm going to tell you something," and I needed that. So, he was a hard-nosed and tough guy, too, but he also had learned when to back off. So, I had a wonderful mentor who, at a very young age, got that through my head and so I had it figured out by the time I was twenty-seven or twenty-eight, because he just beat it out of me. I wasn't mature yet, but I had it figured out.

Washkewicz had the advantage of having several really good mentors, but shares a story of one who was not:

When I was a general manager, my CEO at the time came down with the CFO. Of course, they announced that they were making the rounds, and I think I had my operating returns at that year were like 12 or 13 percent. Not bad—15 is what we kind of target. We want to get everybody at 15, so we were about 12 or 13. So they showed up on the scene and I had a very nice presentation of the changes I was making and where we were heading and so forth. He didn't want to hear any of that. He said, "Don, save that." He said, "Tell me right now when you are going to be at fifteen percent?" I said, "Well, I've got the whole presentation I can show you; it's multi-faceted and I think you'll appreciate." "No, we don't want to see all that. Just tell me when the hell you are going to be at 15 percent [P]!" So you can see it was kind of a sad situation we had then, but I said to myself back then, and this goes back to probably in the early 1980s, I said, "I will never ever, ever do that to anybody.

I will never tell you that you better...I will never beat on a table and ask you when are you going to be at 15 percent? If I can't show you how to get there, I've got no business beating on the table. Now, if I show you how to get there, then I expect you to execute and follow through, okay [T+P]? But he didn't come down here to tell me how he was going to help me get there. He was just going to beat on the table and pontificate and ask when in the hell I'm going to get there. And it's likely he didn't know how either.

Marla Phillips reflects, "Something about my past experiences that might have helped me be comfortable on both sides of the balance framework. I was originally in an environment where, if I made a mistake, I wasn't hammered, and so I felt comfortable trying things and also felt comfortable owning up to things, and so I think your experiences in the past make a difference where you are and, then, hopefully, you can experience things that help you shift and learn [T+P]."

Understands That at the Center of Collaboration Is a Personal Comfort with Valuing the Diversity of People, Ideas, and Ways of Thinking

John Pepper recalls,

So when I joined the company, we were in 11 countries; we are now in over 100; we all wore white shirts and ties, and we were, basically, all men and all from the United States [P]. So we had a major opportunity during my tenure in different places to be working in the whole area of diversity and also the reality of everybody mattering. We ran plants then pretty much like plants were run in the 1920s. "You do this"—command and control— well, that's not the way to do it anymore. Not if you want to be the best company and have people who join you really feel like they own the place, and ownership is critical [T+P]—sense of ownership by every person is critical—absolutely critical...The key thing that happened was when we got to the point where diversity really became coterminus with the strategy, we were enormously helped by being global because I think by being global, we really came to realize that there's no way we could serve the diversity of all the consumers that we were serving—five billion—if we weren't diverse ourselves [T+P]. When that clicked, we could increasingly understand what's happening in China because we have people who understand the Chinese culture; people in a work group here, different color, gender; of course, women demonstrating. Can you imagine how much poorer our results would be if we didn't have women in this company today? It's unbelievable.

Bob McDonald emphasizes,

Well, globalization changed everything [T]. I'll never forget the first time I became aware that I was going to be responsible for people who didn't sit next to me. I struggled with all of my leadership behaviors because leadership behaviors historically have been developed to lead people who you are next to. It throws away the book on leadership and you have to start over again because you're leading people who have been socialized a different way than you, have a language different than yours, who you aren't going to see as frequently as you have in the past [T]. I think it, again, forces you to be much more deliberate as a leader, much more thoughtful, and much more reflective to get the most out of those personal interactions that you do have with the person [T+P]. I think a lot about that. But, obviously, as we've talked before, the standard is treat other people the way *they* want to be treated, not treat other people the way *you* want to be treated. That presupposes you know them; that presupposes you know their culture, and you have to work hard at that. That's a full-time job [T].

Jim McNerney shares,

The complexities of globalization—and, I would add, diversity—have affected my view of collaboration. I go back to this simple premise: If I can figure out a way to get the best out of all 160,000 employees here, I'm going to have one heck of a company [T+P]. We're a big company, and we don't want people hiding in the bureaucracy, afraid to peep out and contribute beyond their jobs. That gets to breaking down barriers that you find in non-diverse environments and in global environments where people don't understand each other or feel uncomfortable with one another. So we work hard at making sure the corporate culture encourages us to find the best in each other [T].

At Boeing, we are just as committed to continuous improvement in diversity and inclusion as we are to continuous improvement in our business performance. Like growth and productivity, each fuels the other. The markets we compete in are *very* complicated. We need lots of different ways of looking at the problems they present us with [T]. I've believed for a long time that innovation is usually a team sport, not so often a solo sport despite all the mythology. Innovation comes far more often from a diverse team freely exchanging ideas than it does from a solitary genius or an insulated team with the occasional "aha" moment along the way. That's a major reason why we pursue a culture of inclusion and sharing.

The first time I had a big job outside the United States was when I ran General Electric's Asia business. I got an outside-in view of both my company and my country and a lot of things I'd never really questioned until then. It's not that I wound up ultimately questioning them, but I was able to see them in a much broader perspective, and I think that was a very valuable experience. It broadened me tremendously [T].

John Lechleiter expands on the topic with,

Globalization presents a challenge that goes beyond partnering per se, and the challenge is how to understand cultural differences which, in turn, has a lot to do with diversity [T]. In general, I believe that in order to understand all aspects of a problem, it's important to bring people into the process who represent different points of view—including different cultural aspects. And you need to make sure that your corporate culture fosters an environment where people will offer those different points of view [T+P].

Tom Cody shares,

You can forget about all the noble reasons to be committed to diversity and make absolutely the single most-compelling business case about any corporate change which, in my judgment, is a commitment to diversity and the difference that makes, at least for us [P]. If our business doesn't reflect the real world, we're not going to have much of a business, so it's a big deal for us.

I'll just speak for our business, but the structure that comes from the right side [*power*] of your chart [The Kucia Balance Framework] is sometimes necessary to give people the security to grow so that they can move more to that side [*together*] of the chart [The Kucia Balance Framework] because to the extent that someone, especially as they're coming up in an organization, can view the structure as a help to help him or her reach a success level, that's important because it's that that gives them the freedom to say this is something we're interested in [T+P].

Richard Antoine knows,

We need to have people who understand something about different cultures. So you need people who understand those differences because you can miss talent and you can miss important business decisions [T+P]. I missed it first in Japan. I thought I was pretty well plugged in when I was talking about a plan that I wanted to do with my senior Japanese manager in manufacturing and he went (sucking in), "That will be very difficult." And you know sucking in is not a good sign!

"That will be very difficult" I thought meant "it would be very difficult to do," which I knew. What he was saying in plain English was, "Hell will freeze over first!" "That's what he was telling me. I didn't know that [T]." But once you've lived in a different culture and understand that things are very different here, you're now sensitized to "Okay, this normal approach—this typical American approach may not work in Saudi Arabia or Thailand or wherever, and I have to get some help from the people here trying to figure out how to do that [T+P]." So you're opened up to a new way of thinking. Right?—you become sensitized [T].

Bob McDonald observes,

> There's a whole other continuum of diversity called "the age
> or experience continuum of diversity" [T] where all of us have
> experienced different things, and the leader's got to be cog-
> nizant of that and change their style to be effective with that
> group of people or individuals that are in that group. The chal-
> lenge is that these groups are all different. Every year a new
> group is going to leave the organization—the older ones—and
> a new group is going to join the organization—the younger
> ones—and you're a member of a group yourself. So, you have
> to be aware of your own socialization; you have to be reflective
> of that. You have to be aware of your own age and reflective
> of that, and force yourself to learn new things. You're trying
> to be consistent so that people will trust you in all of those—
> consistent in value, consistent in principle, but different in style.
> Style is different; principle is the same [T+P].

Marla Phillips shares,

> I'd say the generation ahead of me, which is what most of that
> director's team was made of, actually expressed concern about
> these new employees coming in and not having the dedication
> to the company. Yeah, just job hopping from one job to another.
> Loyalty—that's the word—expressing "what's wrong with
> these new employees? They're young and immature and have
> no loyalty and where's their dedication [P]?" It was Bob and I
> who were the younger portion of the group who kind of spoke
> up and said, "You have to kind of take a look at what's shifted
> in corporate America [T]. When you got a job, you were pretty
> much guaranteed you were going to have this job for the rest
> of your life. So in order for them to progress, it was all focused
> on the hierarchy, and how do I get up there. In order for us
> to progress, we look at learning about this and that because
> there might be another opportunity in another company or
> here because I know no one cares about me. I mean, honestly,
> I think they'd lay me off in a heartbeat if it was the bottom line
> [P]. So it was more learning what you could—first of all because

I was interested in it, but also for others so you would be more diversified, and that's how you gained security, so that if you are all of a sudden cut loose, you are more marketable, you can find a job, and that's how we have to support our family. So the older generation is on the right side of the balance framework [P]. I think it's because of the way corporate America was, and the security that was there [the *power/hierarchy* side] and you move up, whereas, over here [the *together/network* side], you don't have that security, and so it forces you to collaborate and network whether you realize you're doing it or not.

Believes That the Challenge of Leading Change Is Not about Leadership in Control, but Leadership in Balance

This leader believes that collaboration is a means to leadership in balance and is comfortable with ambiguity and change and with giving direction and making decisions. This leader blends the use of data with good judgment and, oftentimes, intuition and instinct to skillfully balance the seeming competing forces of continuity and change and of competition and collaboration as driven by the external forces of market and guided by the internal values of mission and purpose.

John Pepper observes,

The best leaders I've ever known have this wonderful combination of really being anxious to listen and hear what other people have to say and take it all in, and yet have a strong enough sense of themselves to having taken it all in and gone back and forth in an open-minded debate. They'll still come down and say, "This is where I am [T+P]." Make a decision with a strong inward compass of what that decision ought to be without a trace of defensiveness in taking other people's ideas [T+P]. So those are the characteristics that I've seen in great leaders. A. G. Lafley is one of them; John Smale; Rick Levin, president of Yale; Bob Iger at Disney is one. It's really wonderful to see. I think Bob Iger is humble and all of that; he's very down-to-earth, and you can say anything to him. You can just say stuff that some CEOs would say, "Wait a minute. What do you mean by that?" They fight back—they have the tendency to fight back. He doesn't do that. If he thinks it's wrong, he'll say so politely. "Yeah, I hear that; I'll think about that; that's a good point." And he may come back totally on the other side, but he takes it in and considers it. I think he'd agree with the concepts of leadership in balance. I think he'd look at it and say, "I see a lot of myself and what I'm trying to do in there."

Jim McNerney responded,

Do I think I'm in control? Not always. Let's put it this way. The things I like to control have to do with shaping the big picture—the company's culture, the work environment, the course we're on. I don't have to control every tollgate along the way. I think judgment and intuition come into play, especially in "finding a way," one of the Boeing leadership attributes. How do you know that things aren't going well? There's a lot of intuition involved. It involves a lot of staring into people's eyes as they talk to you. It involves judgment. Figuring out what can be fixed and what can't be fixed is based a lot on experience and understanding of people. There's a lot more involved, as you're trying to scramble and find a way to deliver, even though the plan is less relevant than it used to be [T+P].

McNerney observes,

I like the "leader-in-balance" concept. It sounds like you're on to something. It suggests that things are not antagonistic, even if they seem paradoxical [T]. To be a leader you have to be both tough *and* inspirational, far-seeing *and* results-oriented, unsparingly honest *and* strongly supportive. I think the tension between contrasting leadership attributes—those paradoxes— can work well. For example, Jack Welch sent me out to be GE's Asia leader in the early 1990s. He didn't give me a blueprint. He just said, "Asia's the biggest opportunity we've got, and we're not doing enough—so go figure it out." That was typical Jack—both tough *and* inspirational. It was a tremendous learning and growth experience for me. Effective leadership means learning to strike that balance between qualities that may seem contradictory.

I can talk about any issue that I want with anybody, so I try to use power that way—the power to convene, the power of the agenda. But then, after that, I have to rely on my personal effectiveness [T+P]. If I just rely on command and control, I will lose the authenticity and credibility that is so important. In today's world, people aren't going to put up with—nor should they put up with—people who depend on hierarchy for decision making. So every time I make a decision, I feel like I've got to convince somebody no matter what our difference in the hierarchy is. I think that creates the kind of environment I want that is open, collaborative, hard-hitting, facing reality, addressing the tough questions. I think you're not only more likely to get the right answers, but you'll also have a more committed group when you get there [T+P].

Now, there are times when I've just got to say, "Hey, listen— either I don't get it or you don't get it, but I'm the chairman, so we'll do it my way." I win but, again, I sort of eat into my equity when I do that. I don't want to make too much of a habit of that. It's a judgment call [P] on how you do it. There are times when I know that I don't want to spend two hours convincing somebody that they're way off course, so I'll have some fun with it. But, you know, I just cajole them and get other people to help tell them. I think someone in my position has to be seen as someone that others can walk up to and engage in a discussion. To the extent that you have barriers between yourself and others, you lose that interaction that can cause growth [T]. But there's a need for counter-balancing, too. Just because we're collaborative and just because we're trying to help each other grow doesn't mean we're not accountable for results. I try to model that behavior, as well [T+P].

Bob Kohlhepp shared,

There are a handful of times when I ran this company where everybody on the executive committee told me to turn right and

I turned left [P]. Okay? I tell them "this doesn't happen very often." If it happens often, you've got the wrong people working for you or you're a bad leader, but there are a handful of times, and I've seen Dick do the same thing, when everybody told me we ought to do this. I said, "I've heard everything you said; I've thought about it; this is one of those times when I disagree with you; here's what we're going to do and, by God, I expect you to follow me." Then, you're using your position [P].

I am looked upon here as a person who has very strong convictions and will absolutely be unbendable on certain things, but I'm also looked upon as a person who will listen and who will change and so, to me, I think what you're talking about is the balance [T+P]. That's a hard thing for somebody to do—to have that balance of being hard-nosed and being tough and demanding results—but, at the same time, recognizing there's a time to be tough and there's a time not to be tough, and it's an art. You can't read it in a book; it's sort of almost a sense; "this is a time to back off [T]."

John Lechleiter believes,

Intuition is for real. I call it a "tummy feel" for certain things, and I never ignore it [T]. Now, I may override it consciously, but I wish I had a dime for every time that the little bell went off and made me ask, "Is there smoke here? What's wrong with this?" Or, "Why do I know that this is the best way to do this sort of thing?" I can't explain it. I think some of it is just experience, perhaps life experience, in dealing with people. Some of it might be industry experience, although I'll bet that I could go work in another industry and still hear those same bells go off. Personally, I think it's a function of reflection to some extent. I've heard brilliant people argue violently that intuition is the way you should not do things. They will tell you that you should be entirely data driven. I think that we're talking about a different kind of data, that's all. It's information, though it may not be about "net present value" or "return on investment" or the other metrics we typically look at. I look at a lot of that stuff and still think, "That's interesting input, but it's not the only basis on which I'm going to make a decision [T]."

Lechleiter continues,

> As for the things that are "life and death," I like to think long
> and hard. I like to take a long walk and turn the decision over in
> my mind [T]. Sometimes, if your mind is prepared to reflect on
> a decision, then you end up discovering something that causes
> you to see the problem in a new light. I can't tell you how many
> times I've thought, "We've got to do this or that," only to reach
> a different decision on the basis of fresh insight from another
> source, say, an article in the newspaper or something from a
> book.
>
> Experience counts. The Jesuits like to say, "The root of wisdom
> is experience that's reflected upon." Most people have experi-
> ence that they never reflect upon, so it doesn't really count for
> much [T].

Richard Antoine points out,

> That's the hard thing about leadership. Sometimes you can't
> have all the data you would like to have, and sometimes you've
> got trusted people. I mean the rest of the people here aren't
> smarter or dumber than anybody else. They just have a totally
> different view of it. You have to make a decision that you think
> is right and then, after you make it, there's no turning back [P].
> One of the things I've seen about A. G. or other good leaders
> is they're willing to make the decision and then they're on to
> something else. A lot of the rest of us might be worrying and
> wondering, "How is this thing going to work out. Because once
> you start making the change, you're done, right?" Everybody's
> working from the same data with very different conclusions and
> the herd mentality is usually—all I take consolation in is the
> consensus is usually the wrong answer. I don't know what the
> right one is, but the consensus is usually the wrong answer on
> those kinds of things [P].
>
> But the facts are the same. No one, I don't think—very few
> people—have extra facts. It's all a matter of how you interpret
> those facts and how you integrate the various things that are
> going on around the world. I think great leaders are able to

come up with different ways, or different conclusions, that lead to executions, and this predictive thing is really important. So I don't know. I'd say we're a mixture. Our effective leaders are a mixture of this—*together* and *power* [T+P].

A Reflection

Leadership in balance is not a style of leadership, it is leadership with style—a personal style—that begins with the way of thinking, the way of understanding and being that forms the foundation for a leader's decisions and actions. While these leaders are each very different people with different personalities challenged with leading different types of organizations and businesses, there is something in common about the way they think. They think like *leaders in balance*.

Chapter 10

The Research Foundation for Leadership in Balance

It was in the spirit of Peter Senge's observation that "from experience rather than concepts" come the most profound, yet simple, ideas that led John Kucia to join with Fr. Michael Graham, S. J., president of Xavier University, and A. G. Lafley, CEO of Procter & Gamble, to pursue a doctoral dissertation titled, "Leadership in Balance: The Role of Collaboration for Leading Change in a Living Organization."

Kucia began his journey using qualitative-research methods and the case-study approach to explore and describe the process of collaboration in both a for-profit corporation and a university.

Along his research journey, Kucia discovered clear indications that universities are being pushed to become more businesslike, with more focus, accountability and connection to the business world. Corporations, by contrast, were becoming more collaborative and leaders were being encouraged to build and foster trusting relationships and corporate community. These findings compelled Kucia to pursue a clear definition of purpose-driven collaboration as a means to establishing learning and work communities that create better strategies for a long life.

One of the outcomes of Kucia's research is "The DNA of Collaboration: The Kucia Balance Framework" first introduced in chapter 4. This model describes a collaborative leader who can balance the competing forces of continuity and change and competition and collaboration, as driven by the external forces of the market and guided by the internal values of mission and purpose.

The Kucia Balance Framework model serves as a foundation for the next level of Kucia's original research, The Eight Ways of Thinking, introduced in chapter 3. He derived these ways of thinking by thoughtfully reviewing the original transcripts of approximately 30 interviews with Procter & Gamble executives and Xavier trustees. As a result, Kucia identified eight common ways of thinking across that initial group of participants.

When we began collaboration for this book, we decided to develop an instrument that would support us in the interview process with top executives in successful, long-lived organizations around the country. The initial instrument that Gravett developed was crafted to capture whether seasoned leaders resonated with the eight ways of thinking and to what degree of intensity. Knowing that busy executives have limited time and energy to complete assessments, the instrument was limited to 24 items.

The short-form assessment was administered to approximately 30 senior-level executives, who found the instrument to be clear and relatively easy to take. From Kucia and Gravett's perspective as researchers, we decided to not share the assessment results with our interviewees after an executive interview early in the process focused undue attention and conversation on their score.

To minimize the likelihood that future assessment takers would focus too much on simply scoring well relative to other leaders, we asked an industrial-organizational (I-O) psychologist on staff at Xavier University, Dr. Phillip Jones, to develop a 40-item version of the assessment that could be used for leaders at all levels within diverse organizations. An excerpt from the assessment that Dr. Jones developed is shown in Appendix 1. The focus, we hoped, would be on what leaders actually thought and how they responded to leadership dilemmas, as opposed to having the "right" answer. Appendix 2 contains an excerpt from the short form assessment developed by Kucia and Gravett.

Since we interviewed and provided an assessment for our original research group, we have given both assessments to leaders at all levels in many organizations around the country through Gravett's executive coaching practice. Since 2009, we have also provided the assessment to leaders who are students in Xavier University's Leadership Institute. A natural question is if the short form and the long form essentially and equally measure our concept of leadership. In order to assess the degree of equality among the two measures, we sought to verify that the two assessments were correlated and had convergent validity. We elected to invite a research team of graduate I-O psychology graduate students at Xavier to conduct an independent study. This technical team, to which we are very grateful, was led by Dr. Dalia Diab and assisted by Dr. Mark Nagy. The names of all class members are listed in the Acknowledgement section of this book.

In the remainder of this chapter, we are sharing their results substantiating that our short- and long-form instruments are essentially equivalent and correlated with one another.

Evidence of Validity

One question that must be answered when evaluating two forms of the same leadership model is if the same eight leadership dimensions are related to each other. The results of the study clearly showed this to be the case. Based on the results of their study, the technical report team found that the overall scores were consistent among the dimensions of both forms. Importantly, each long-form leadership dimension was significantly correlated with the corresponding short-form leadership dimension. This is clear evidence of validity and indicates that however the leadership dimension is measured, whether via the short form of the long form, one can be confident in obtaining similar results.

Interestingly, correlations between the short- and long-form were more strongly related among dimensions 5 through 8 than between dimensions 1 through 4. Specifically, these are the correlations between the short- and long-form leadership dimensions are as shown in table 10.1. Again, all of the correlations were statistically significant.

We were also pleased to discover that all but two of the remaining correlations (103 out of 105) were statistically significant; the only correlations that were not significant were between the long-form dimension 4 and short-form dimension 6 and between long-form dimension 4 and short-form dimension 7. These significant correlations among the leadership dimensions across the short and long forms indicate that these dimensions likely represent the overall construct of leadership.

Table 10.1 Correlations between eight dimensions on short and long form assessments

Dimension	Correlation (r)
1. Approaches leadership as a relationship not a position	0.46
2. Understands that the leader embodies the brand promise	0.43
3. Is motivated by a higher purpose, a mission, and believes that mission drives the numbers	0.41
4. Understands collaboration must have a business purpose	0.35
5. Thinks outside of the pyramid in order to share power and spread leadership, authority and responsibility throughout the organization	0.76
6. Believes teaching and leadership have a great deal in common	0.72
7. Understands that at the center of collaboration is a personal comfort with valuing the diversity of people, ideas, and ways of thinking	0.80
8. Believes that the challenge of leading change is not about leadership in control, but leadership in balance	0.83

A second question that also must be answered is whether the leadership instrument yields scores that are indicative of leadership performance. That is, a leadership instrument based on a solid leadership model should produce scores that differentiate those in higher organizational positions from those in lower organizational positions. Following the interviews with CEOs for the original research, Gravett has administered both assessments to leaders at all organizational levels, for students in Xavier University's Leadership Institute and for Gravett's coaching clients. Therefore, the technical team analyzed the results of each form's total score using a one-way analysis (ANOVA) to examine the relationship between managerial- and top-leadership-level thinking. (See Appendix 3 for the ANOVA results.) Results showed that there was a significant difference in how managers at different organizational levels scored on leadership thinking in both the short and long forms.

Each level of management was given a ranking based on the score received on both forms, with "1" representing the highest score and "7" representing the lowest score. As one would expect from a valid leadership assessment, CEOs had the highest means on both forms and were most-closely aligned with The Eight Ways of Thinking model. Further, the technical team also conducted post hoc comparisons using Tukey's Honestly Significant Difference (HSD) procedure. Results revealed that on both the short and long forms, mid-level managers scored significantly lower than directors and presidents.

Additionally, directors and CFOs scored significantly lower than CEOs on the short form, which indicates that the short form may be a slightly better leadership assessment than the long form. Across both forms, mid-level managers always ranked last and CEOs always ranked first. Interestingly, the president and COO switched rankings between forms. In the short form, COOs and presidents ranked third and fourth, respectively, and in the long form, they ranked fourth and third, respectively.

The technical team's conclusion was that the overall results indicated that the leadership self-assessment scores seemed to be consistent in measuring the leadership qualities on each dimension. Moreover, the corresponding dimensions on the long and short forms were significantly correlated with each other, yet dimensions 1–4 yielded low to moderate correlations between forms, whereas dimensions 5–8 yielded high correlations between the forms.

Again, as one should expect with a valid leadership assessment, mid-level managers scored lower on all leadership dimensions compared to the higher-level managers. The difference between mid-level managers and CFOs was statistically significant on the short form. However, this difference was not statistically significant on the long form. Because of this finding, the short form may be better at differentiating between mid-level managers and CFOs, directors and CEOs, and CEOs and CFOs.

Our technical team suggested that there are several applications for the short- and long-form assessments in organizations. For instance, The Eight Ways of Thinking instrument could be used to help select and/or promote individuals into all types of leadership positions. For those already in the organization, the model may be used as a professional development tool to provide helpful guidance to not only improve leader performance, but also to enhance retention. We agree, and plan to continue tweaking and administering the assessments to leaders who are interested in becoming leaders in balance.

Chapter 11

The Fundamental Shift: Capstone Thoughts

The central message of this book is that the leadership required for a living organization in the twenty-first century calls for new habits of the mind. This a fundamental shift from emphasis on leadership in control to leadership in balance and from a leader's ways of behaving to a leader's ways of thinking. Through the chapters of this book, we have discovered important new thinking that adds value to the study and practice of leadership in a twenty-first century global society.

Throughout this book, you have heard and learned from real leaders in balance. They are individuals capable of leading long-living organizations. They are people who think critically and reflectively with the *head of a strategist* who make decisions with a *moral and ethical heart* and who execute strategy with the *hand of a collaborative leader*.

Leaders in balance are individuals best suited to lead an organization that will survive for a hundred years or more. They lead in a collaborative manner and create a culture and structure that nurture and grow their organizations of talented people. Their organizations are capable of learning and governing their own growth and evolution; of building community and a persona on the inside; and of building constructive relationships inside and outside of the organization. This is not a description of the ideal leader. This is the profile of leaders needed at all levels of all organizations, whether for-profit or not-for-profit.

We know that leaders are built from the inside out. The way a leader thinks deserves our critical attention. Why? Because what a leader sees and how he or she understands and interprets meaning to their organization gives rise to the strategies, decisions, and actions of the leader and the future direction of the organization. A leader's way of thinking precedes action and sets the course for their organization. We have worked to discover the ways of thinking of successful people who understand that in this complex global world their leadership challenge is one of balance not control.

We have developed The Kucia Balance Framework to depict the art of collaborative leadership. We chose the DNA metaphor and the double helix to describe the interdependence and the complementary (balance) relationship between collaboration and command-and-control forms of leadership. The balance framework is a conceptual guide that enables the leader to first recognize, then reflect, and, finally, understand the leadership challenge at hand. The Eight Ways of Thinking inform, animate, and bring life to the good judgment, the intuition, and the balance that gives rise to a leader's ways of behaving. The Kucia Balance Framework[1] and The Eight Ways of Thinking are new mental models and valuable tools for the mind. They do not provide the answer. Like the *Tao*, they offer a way to the answer. It is important to note that collaboration is not consensus building; collaboration is a means to an end. Collaboration is a purpose-driven effort that leads to better solutions, better strategies, and better execution.

We have confirmed that leaders in balance share common ways of thinking that ultimately pave the way to their behavior. A leader in balance understands that leadership is a relationship that embodies the brand promise motivated by a higher purpose. Collaboration must have a business purpose that shares power and authority. A leader in balance also believes leading has much in common with teaching, values diversity, and leads change rather than controls it.

We offer a few observations to add to what we have learned. Taken together, five of the eight ways of thinking—first, second, fourth, fifth, and sixth—create a strong core—a blend of *head*, *heart*, and *hand* representing a foundation of an integrated leader in balance. These ways of thinking were most strongly evident among our corporate participants.

Although the third, seventh, and eighth ways of thinking were prominent among our participants, they seemed to present more of a challenge worth briefly exploring.

Regarding the third way of thinking, it is difficult to balance being bottom-line driven (and all that is represented on the *power* side of the balance framework) with being mission driven. Most organizations—for-profit and not-for-profit—have a mission to serve some population or public good. For most, the first marker of performance and success begins and ends with profits and topline and bottom-line growth. All other success criteria seem to support the first.

In the seventh way of thinking, personal comfort with valuing diversity is another key component at the center of collaboration. Many say they value diversity, but struggle to better understand and to become comfortable with the many dimensions of diversity. Embracing diversity adds an enriching and powerful force to an organization that encourages innovation and creativity. Diversity releases energy and spreads influence, power and authority—some of the basic goals of leadership in balance as displayed on the *together* side of the balance framework.

One interpretation for the eighth way of thinking could relate to the difficulty in dealing with the topic of control. None of the participants really believes she/he can successfully lead an organization alone. None believed she/he was in control; and all participants acknowledged they need the good work of others to be successful. So they may, in their hearts, know they are not in control, but struggle with how to live with this fact. Hence, the value of remaining in balance on the inside—mindful and intentional, open and aware, calm and clear, taking action as needed, centered, intuitive in clear-minded response to the situation—is accomplished by adopting and adapting to the seven other ways of thinking of a leader in balance as informed by The Kucia Balance Framework.

The balance framework also describes an emerging organizational structure—the network. Purpose-driven networks of talented people can be formed to address the challenges of change (growth and learning) versus routine organizational activities (keeping the trains running on time) best served by the hierarchy.

We understand the way the hierarchy works. It is the structure through which command-and-control behaviors are practiced. Networks change the structure of an organization thereby changing the relationships and behaviors among people, the processes and outcomes, and, eventually, the culture of an organization. The together side of the balance framework suggests how networks can encourage diversity of thought, innovation, and creativity; spread influence and power; and that can organize learning communities and produce disciplined people, thought, and action. Instead of replacing the hierarchy, networks can be used to augment it and to encourage a culture and practice of collaboration.

Since the functioning of the network is less controlled, it is more difficult to envision it as a viable organizational structure. A frequent question posed about the use of networks is, "Who's in charge?" The answer is, "That depends on the issue." At the center of collaboration and networks must be a leader who is comfortable with spreading control and influence, a person who values a diversity of people and ideas. Networks can be a source of much talent, innovation, learning, and energy when organized around a purpose and a desired result.

And finally, as leaders in balance, we understand that the world is a large living system. A cell, a human, a community, a corporation, a nation, and the world are all living systems. We know that true learning only occurs when there is a change of mind, a shift in thinking. This change occurs first in the mind of an individual and only then does that shift in thinking influence the organization and ultimately a civilization. This suggests the primacy and importance of individual reflection and learning.

To develop and connect this thinking in a more concrete and tangible form, we offer figure 11.1 that depicts these concepts.

The human systems diagram (figure 11.1)[2] suggests that change occurs first in the mind of an individual and only then does that shift influence the organization and ultimately civilization. Change is first dependent upon the way individuals think, what they see, and how they understand and interpret meaning, which paves the way for the preferences, values, and priorities of the organizations. It is through institutions that much of the work of society is conducted. Further, this diagram

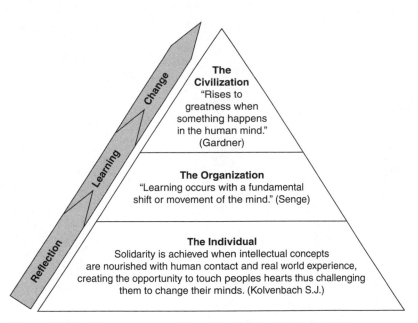

Figure 11.1 Human systems. Copyright © John F. Kucia, 2004.

suggests the importance and value of the way one thinks, the individual reflection and learning in the process of change as it impacts organizations and, ultimately, civilization.

To accomplish that end, collaboration serves as a tool, a means to achieve balance for a person who leads, with the head of strategist, with a moral and ethical heart, and with the hand of a collaborative leader. Such leadership is critical for organizational success in today's competitive and rapidly changing global marketplace. It is in discovering the common ground, rather than focusing on the differences, that individuals, leaders, institutions, and corporations must bond in a collaborative fashion to accomplish their special missions and to better serve society.

Appendix 1

Self-Assessment: A Leader in Balance—The Eight Ways of Thinking

For each pair of items select (check) alternative A or B that more closely reflects what you believe or what you do. Even if both alternatives reflect your thinking or behavior, select only the one alternative that is more closely like you.

1A. ____ Two phrases that could well describe me in difficult times or situations are, "When the going gets tough, the tough get going," and "Never let them see you sweat."

1B. ____ In difficult times or situations, I find it easy to turn to others for help.

2A. ____ Good leaders become that way through their willingness to prepare, take risks, and work harder than most others.

2B. ____ Much of the success attributed to me should really be attributed to others around me and in support of me.

3A. ____ People describe me as a good listener.

3B. ____ People describe me as decisive.

4A. ____ I believe most of my decisions are mission based, long term in nature.

4B. ____ I believe most of my decisions, while keeping the mission in mind, are dealing with shorter-term issues.

5A._____ I believe it is important for each individual in an organization to have a plan for professional growth and development and for them to seek mentors and coaches to help them achieve that plan.

5B._____ For my direct reports, I serve as a mentor and a coach personally involved in ensuring their professional growth.

Appendix 2

Self-Assessment: A Leader in Balance—Short Form

For each item, place the most accurate response to the left of each number.

1. Rarely
2. Occasionally
3. Sometimes
4. Usually
5. Almost always

____1. I consider implications for my organization's future with each decision I make.

____2. I ask people to follow me because they trust and respect me, not because of my position.

____3. I build relationships inside my organization with people who add value to my strengths.

____4. I take intentional "time outs" to reflect on aligning my personal objectives and values with organizational values.

____5. I establish success criteria for key result areas necessary for our organization to survive.

Appendix 3

ANOVA Results

Table A3.1 Overall means and standard deviations for the long- and short-form dimensions

Variable	M	SD
SF Dimension 1	12.80	1.59
SF Dimension 2	12.60	1.69
SF Dimension 3	12.59	1.71
SF Dimension 4	12.64	1.70
SF Dimension 5	12.64	1.80
SF Dimension 6	12.76	1.69
SF Dimension 7	12.80	1.62
SF Dimension 8	13.03	1.60
SF total	**101.65**	**9.93**
LF Dimension 1	3.79	0.86
LF Dimension 2	3.70	0.88
LF Dimension 3	3.74	0.90
LF Dimension 4	3.56	1.20
LF Dimension 5	3.66	1.13
LF Dimension 6	3.70	1.11
LF Dimension 7	3.61	1.15
LF Dimension 8	3.73	1.20
LF total	**29.55**	**5.83**

Note: D = Dimension; $N = 197$; SF = short form; LF = long form.

Table A3.2 Correlations among all dimensions and total scores between the two forms

Variable	1	2	3	4	5	6
1 SF Dimension 1						
2 SF Dimension 2	.78					
3 SF Dimension 3	.59	.71				
4 SF Dimension 4	.51	.52	.64			
5 SF Dimension 5	.50	.46	.46	.56		
6 SF Dimension 6	.49	.39	.31	.34	.52	
7 SF Dimension 7	.43	.42	.36	.35	.31	.54
8 SF Dimension 8	.61	.59	.49	.39	.41	.38
9 SF total	.82	.81	.75	.72	.71	.65
10 LF Dimension 1	**.46**	.49	.47	.44	.49	.35
11 LF Dimension 2	.44	**.43**	.41	.36	.37	.37
12 LF Dimension 3	.46	.43	**.41**	.29	.32	.37
13 LF Dimension 4	.36	.45	.36	**.35**	.29	*.08*
14 LF Dimension 5	.49	.47	.47	.53	**.76**	.45
15 LF Dimension 6	.51	.48	.43	.42	.52	**.72**
16 LF Dimension 7	.54	.51	.46	.41	.44	.54
17 LF Dimension 8	.67	.60	.53	.45	.45	.47
18 LF total	.71	.70	.64	.59	.65	.60

Note: $N = 197$; SF = short form; LF = long form. All correlations are statistically significant, $p < .01$, except for the two italicized correlations. The boldfaced correlations signify the correlations of the corresponding dimensions between the two forms.

7	8	9	10	11	12	13	14	15	16	17
.51										
.63	.73									
.27	.43	.59								
.29	.34	.52	.50							
.27	.34	.50	.39	.48						
.12	.24	.41	.41	.36	.31					
.28	.34	.64	.47	.38	.37	.35				
.44	.37	.64	.39	.35	.30	.20	.54			
.80	.56	.70	.44	.38	.41	.25	.39	.54		
.49	**.83**	.76	.51	.39	.45	.36	.44	.48	.59	
.54	.63	.86	.72	.66	.65	.60	.72	.69	.72	.77

Table A3.3 One-way between-subjects ANOVA results for the short-form and the long-form total scores

Source	SS	df	MS	F	p	η^2
Short form						
Between groups	12002.13	6	2000.36	51.87	< .001	.62
Within groups	7326.70	190	38.56			
Total	19328.83	196				
Long form						
Between groups	2594.47	6	432.41	20.24	< .001	.39
Within groups	4058.22	190	21.36			
Total	6652.69	196				

Note: SS: Sum of Squares; df: degrees of freedom; MS: Mean Square; F: F-ratio; p: p-value; η2: eta squared.

Table A3.4 Means and standard deviations for the long- and short-form total scores by managerial level

Managerial level	M	SD	N
Short form			
Mid-level manager	93.01	6.84	85
Director	106.10	6.14	41
VP	109.08	5.33	13
CEO	112.58	3.56	24
CFO	102.00	7.52	5
COO	108.60	5.17	10
President	108.05	6.60	19
Long form			
Mid-level manager	25.49	5.17	85
Director	31.54	4.99	41
VP	33.38	4.57	13
CEO	34.00	2.54	24
CFO	30.60	4.28	5
COO	32.60	1.96	10
President	33.32	4.15	19

Notes

Introduction

1. Peter Senge, Bryan Smith, Nina Kruschwitz, Joe Laur, and Sara Schley, *The Necessary Revolution* (New York: Doubleday 2008), 8–12.
2. John Kucia, "The DNA of Collaboration: The Kucia Balance Framework," in "Leadership in Balance: The Role of Collaboration for Leading Change in a Living Organization," EdD diss., University of Pennsylvania Graduate School of Education, 2004.
3. Gary Hamel, *The Future of Management* (Boston: Harvard Business Press, 2007), 3, 11, 183, 244.
4. Noel Tichy and Warren Bennis, *Judgment: How Winning Leaders Make Great Calls* (New York: Portfolio Penguin Group, 2007), 4–18.
5. Don Tapscott and Anthony D. Williams, *Wikinomics: How Mass Collaboration Changes Everything* (New York: Portfolio Penguin Group, 2006), 3–18.
6. Tapscott and Williams, "Collaborative Minds: The Power of Thinking Differently," in *Wikinomics*, 270, 289–290.
7. Peter Senge, C. Otto Sharmer, Joseph Jawarsky, and Betty Sue Flowers, *Presence: An Exploration of Profound Change in People, Organizations and Society* (New York: Crown Business, 2004), 15.
8. Arie de Geus, *The Living Company* (Boston: Harvard Business Press, 1996), 1–12.
9. Richard Boyatzis and Annie McKee, *Resonant Leadership* (Boston: Harvard Business Press, 2005), x, 4, 227–229.

10. Thomas Friedman, *The World Is Flat* (New York: Farrar, Strauss and Giroux, 2005), 48–172, 175, 201, 213, 352.
11. Thomas Friedman, *The Lexus and the Olive Tree: Understanding Globalization* (New York: Farrar, Strauss and Giroux, 1999).
12. Friedman, *The World Is Flat*.
13. Justin Menkes, *Executive Intelligence* (New York: Harper Collins, 2005).

1   Leader as Brand

1. John Kucia, "Leader as Brand," in "Leadership in Balance: The Role of Collaboration for Leading Change in a Living Organization," EdD diss., University of Pennsylvania Graduate School of Education, 2004.

2   A New Model of Leadership for a Living Organization

1. Arie de Gues, *The Living Company* (Boston: Harvard Press, 1996), 1–12.
2. John Kucia, "Leadership in Balance: The Role of Collaboration for Leading Change in a Living Organization," EdD diss., University of Pennsylvania Graduate School of Education, 2004, 66–72.
3. John Kucia, "The DNA of Collaboration: The Kucia Balance Framework," in "Leadership in Balance: The Role of Collaboration for Leading Change in a Living Organization," EdD diss., University of Pennsylvania Graduate School of Education, 2004, 65.

3   It's Time for a Different Leadership Paradigm

1. Linda Gravett and Robin Throckmorton, *Bridging the Generation Gap* (New Jersey: Career Press, 2007).
2. Marcus Buckingham and Curt Coffman, *First, Break All the Rules* (New York: Simon & Schuster, 1999).
3. Richard Boyatzis and Annie McKee, *Resonant Leadership* (Boston: Harvard Business Press, 2005).
4. Linda Gravett and Sheri Caldwell, *Using Your Emotional Intelligence to Develop Others* (New York: Palgrave Macmillan, 2009).

5. James Collins, *Good to Great: Why Some Companies Make the Leap and Others Don't* (New York: Harper Business Press, 2001).

6. John Kucia, "The DNA of Collaboration: The Kucia Balance Framework," in "Leadership in Balance: The Role of Collaboration for Leading Change in a Living Organization," EdD diss., University of Pennsylvania Graduate School of Education, 2004, 96.

7. Bart Sayle and Surinder Kumar, *Riding the Blue Train* (New York: Penguin Group, 2006), 8–9.

4 The Structure of the Ways of Leaders in Balance

1. John Kucia, "Leadership in Balance: The Role of Collaboration for Leading Change in a Living Organization," EdD diss., University of Pennsylvania Graduate School of Education, 2004, 59.

2. Kucia, "Leadership in Balance: The Role of Collaboration for Leading Change in a Living Organization," 61–63.

3. Sun Tzu, translated by James Clavell, *The Art of War* (New York: Dell Publishing, 1983).

4. Morihei Ueshiba, translated by John Stevens, *The Art of Peace* (Boston: Shambhala Publications Inc., 2002), 31–36.

5. Kucia, "Leadership in Balance: The Role of Collaboration for Leading Change in a Living Organization," 93–102.

6. *Nemawashi* (根回し) is the combination of the noun "root" 根 (*ne*) and the transitive verb "to circulate" 回す (*mawasu*). When these two kanji are combined, 回す (*mawasu*) becomes 回し (*mawashi*), and together they create 根回し (*nemawashi*). In the diagram of The DNA of Collaboration: The Kucia Balance Framework in figure 4.3, the two complementary meanings of collaboration discussed in this book—*kyouryoku* and *nemawashi*—are split apart like puzzle pieces into four quadrants containing their kanji and the English words: *together, power, root*, and *circulate*. While the word for "circulate" as a kanji idea standing alone is technically written as 回す, the second half of 根回し, written as 回し, is being used here for cohesive reading and clear comprehension of the *nemawashi* 根回し concept in The Kucia Balance Framework.

5   The Power of Leadership in Balance: The Connection to an Organization's Survival

1. Diane Coutu, *How Resilience Works* (Boston: Harvard Business Review, 2002).

6   New Habits of the Mind: The Ways of a Leader in Balance

1. Daniel Goleman, Richard Boyatzis, and Annie McKee, *Primal Leadership: Learning to Lead with Emotional Intelligence* (Boston: Harvard Business Review Press, 2004).
2. William Torbert, *The Power of Balance* (Newbury Park, CA: SAGE Publications Inc., 1991), 5.
3. Thomas Cleary, *The Book of Balance and Harmony* (Boston: Shambhala Publications Inc., 2003), 2.
4. Sun Tzu, translated by James Clavell, *The Art of War* (New York: Dell Publishing, 1983).
5. Kisshomaru Ueshiba, translated by Taitesu Unno, *The Spirit of Aikido* (Tokyo: Kodansha International, 1984), 42.
6. Morihei Ueshiba, translated by John Stevens, *The Art of Peace* (Boston: Shambhala Publications Inc., 2002), 35.

7   New Behaviors That Correlate to The Eight Ways of Thinking

1. Robert Kaplan and David Norton, *The Balanced Scorecard: Translating Strategy into Action* (Boston: Harvard Business Review, 1996).
2. Marcus Buckingham and Curt Coffman, *First, Break All the Rules* (New York: Simon & Schuster, 1999).
3. Michael Zwell, *Creating a Culture of Competence* (New York: John Wiley & Sons, 2000).

11   The Fundamental Shift: Capstone Thoughts

1. John Kucia, "Leadership in Balance: The Role of Collaboration for Leading Change in a Living Organization," EdD diss., University of Pennsylvania Graduate School of Education, 2004, 103–104.
2. Peter Hans Kolvenbach, "The Service of Faith and the Promotion of Justice in American Higher Education," presented at the Conference of Jesuit Educators, Santa Clara

University, Santa Clara, California, October 6, 2000, 7; Peter Senge, *The Fifth Discipline: The Art and Practice of the Learning Organization* (New York: Currency Doubleday, 1990), 13; and John Gardner, *On Leadership* (New York: Free Press, 1993), 13.

Index

Aikido, 81, 166
Antoine, Dick, 125, 135, 141
Art of Peace, The, 54, 81
Art of War, The, 52, 80
Artz, Ed, 15
assumptions, 24, 35, 44, 79

Baby Boomers
    Gen X and Gen Y, 27, 83, 107
balance
    means for achieving, 46
    notion of, the, 35, 55
    power of, the, 78
Ballon, S. J., Robert, 46
behaviors
    breakthrough, 36, 38–9
    changes, 40
    coaching and mentoring, 38
    a different set of, 35
    intentional, 99
    model, 30
    new, 44, 87, 89, 91, 93, 95, 97,
        99, 101–3, 166
    principles around, 90
    that embody the brand promise,
        91
Boeing Leadership Center, 111,
    124
brand
    of collaborative leader, 52, 74
    leader as, 3, 74, 164
    personal, 46, 52, 59, 74
    promise, 4, 8, 18, 23, 73, 75,
        91–2, 119, 122, 150

branding
    points of sameness and the points
        of difference, 92
    power of, 3
bricolage, approach to reasoning by
    analogy, 50

Capstone thoughts, 149, 166
Castellini, Bob, 67, 114
challenges
    court, 100
    distribution, 111
    insights into, 102, 118
    paradoxical, 45–6, 50
    range of, 35, 55
change
    acceptance of policy, 43
    catalyst, 34
    and change, 46, 137, 144
    challenges of, 57, 75, 152
    as a constant, 40
    culture, 113
    groundwork for impending
        change, 42
    implementing, 113
    incremental, 39, 52–4, 78
    leading, 4, 13, 15, 23, 45, 77–8,
        100, 119, 137, 143, 146, 163–6
    nurturing change effort, 44, 54
    positive, 67–8
    prepare for, 47, 125
    process, 42–4
    quantum, 54
    in societal norms, 42

change—*Continued*
  stages of, 41, 113
  times of, 39
Chung, Peter, 26
Cleary, Thomas, 79, 166
Cody, Tom, 24, 95–6, 114, 135
collaboration
  Asian concepts of, 49
  critical skill, 126
  culture of, 18, 53
  execution of, 56
  is harder than command and
    control, 125
  horizontal capabilities, 8
  importance of collaboration, 128
  and networks, 152
  new set of skills required, 127
  notion of, the, 16, 49
  purpose-driven, 17, 51, 75–6, 125
Collaboration Equation, The
  business purpose, 21, 23, 49–51, 56,
    59–60, 76, 93–4, 119, 125, 150
collaborative leader
  authentic and a pragmatist, 16
  believes teaching and leadership
    have a great deal in common,
    19, 23, 77, 97, 119, 129, 146
  characteristics of, 21
  hand of a, 21, 61, 119, 149, 154
  in a living organization, 56
Collins, Jim, 34, 97
command and control, 25, 52–4,
    80, 98, 150, 152
  approach is a symptom of serious
    organizational issues, 30
  authority, 54
  behaviors, 152
  forms of leadership, 150
  hierarchy, 52, 80
  lose authenticity and credibility,
    90, 139
  system, 54
  type of leader, 98
commitment
  building commitment phases, 113

building to change, 41–3
to diversity, 135
communication
  across divisions, 31
  central message, 149
  Communications Model, The,
    108
  company, 65
  continuous cross-functionally,
    111
  face-to-face, 70, 108
  keep lines open at all levels, 24
  written, 89
community
  ability to build, 21, 61, 119
  camaraderie around fulfilling the
    mission, 90
  collaborative, 19, 77, 98
  global, 33, 64
competencies
  applied, 35
  collaborative, 82
  critical, 63
  different, 54
  eight core, 23
  essential, 44
  genetic, 56
  groupings of, 52
  key, 39
  new, 20, 40, 77
  performance, 90
  technical, 12
concepts
  and change, 46, 137, 144
  classroom, 33
  a critical thinker uses, 24
  from experience rather than, 143
  intellectual, 153
  root and circulate, 47, 51, 59–60
  together and power, 47, 50–1,
    59–60, 78, 142
  versus change, 45, 50
continuity
  challenge of balancing with
    change, 18

and change, 46, 137, 144
competing forces, 137, 144
leadership-continuity plans and
    initiatives, 29, 95
maintaining, 67
support leadership, 39
through change, 46
transitional, 53
versus change, 45, 50
core values
    establishment of core values, 28
    model for resiliency, 70
corporate
    change, 135
    commitment, 83
    community, 143
    culture, 134
    DNA, 60–1, 127
critical thinking
    engage in, 37
    exercise in, 118
    objective, 34
culture
    audit, 42
    Chinese, 133
    collaborative, 8, 20
    competence, 18, 20, 77
    of competition, 53
    differences, 134
    different, 30, 99, 135
    Eastern and Western, 53
    of inclusion, 134
    of innovation, 55
    Japanese, 59
    of a long-living organization, 50
    of an organization, 20, 111, 152
    organization's, 40, 106, 125

de Gues, Arie, xvi, 15, 164
decision making
    accountability, 109
    collective, 70
    effect, 44
    ethical, 28, 64
    ethical framework, 63

intentional and deliberate, 82
participative, 66
primary guides, 59
process, 34, 112, 126
spreading, 114
unilateral, 25
decisions
    behavior and, 82
    business, 135
    high-integrity, 63
    justification for, 25
    a leader's, 73–4, 142
    making, 17, 52, 75, 78, 100–1,
        106, 111, 137
    sound, 24
    unilateral, 114
directed assignments, 96
diversity
    brings creativity, 99
    at the center of collaboration,
        23, 77, 119, 132, 146,
        151–2
    continuous improvement, 134
    continuum of, 136
    embracing, 25, 151
    encourage, 34, 44, 152
    of ideas, 20, 77
    initiative, 37, 42–3
    managing, 100
    value of, 117
DNA
    classic double helix, 56–7
    DNA of Collaboration, The, 45,
        50–1, 53, 55, 56, 143, 163–5
    East informs West, 45
    genetic code, 56
    ladder, 56–7
    metaphor, 51, 150
Eight Ways of Thinking, The
    brings emotional intelligence to
        leadership, 75
    complementary, 50–1
    Eight Ways of Thinking model,
        147
    genetic, 51

Eight Ways of
    Thinking—*Continued*
  identifying both The Eight Ways
    of Thinking and The Kucia
    Balance Framework in action,
    78, 120
  learning from mentors through,
    117
  of meaningfulness, 38
  new behaviors that correlate to, 87
emotional intelligence
  concept of, 33
  emotional intelligence, 35
  emotional self-control, 34
  learning to lead with, 74, 166
  together with IQ, 8
Engle, Dorothy, 51
Eskew, Mike, 67
ethics
  breaches in, 28
  code of, 64–5, 90
execution
  better, 17, 82, 150
  linking strategy to, 4
  phase, 113
  of the strategy, 49, 60
  successful, 16

failure is learning, 9
Farmer, Dick, 97, 131
Five E's, 128
global markets, 30
globalization
  challenge of, 117–18
  complexities of, 133
  effect of, 99
  market realities of, 7
Graham, J., S. J., Michael, 3, 92,
    100, 112
Green, Lenny, 39
Hans Kolvenbach, Peter, 166
hierarchy
  augment the, 20
  reliance on the, 52
  traditional, 21, 54
Human Systems diagram, 153

Iger, Bob, 31, 137
innovation
  encouraging, 38
  Innovation Initiative, 31
  meritocracy, 67
  promote, 100
  is usually a team sport, 134
intuition, a function of reflection,
    140

kanji
  concept of, deeper meaning of,
    and collaboration, 47–8
  Japanese, 59, 79–80
  root and circulate, 47
  together and power, 55, 78
kinetic energy, 39
Kohlhepp, Bob, 30, 89, 97–8,
    109–10, 121, 125, 130, 139
Kraeutler, Jack, 27, 29–30, 94
Kucia Balance Framework, The
  in action, 105, 120
  an integration of head, heart, and
    hand, 52
  using The Kucia Balance
    Framework as a guide, 102
  utilizing elements of, 105
  a valuable tool, 51
Lafley, A. G., 3, 17, 91, 93, 101,
    137, 143
leader in balance
  actively listens, 71
  adapts quickly to different
    cultures, 30
  behavior of a, 61
  clear on her/his core values, 70
  concepts of, 61, 138
  creates loyalty to the institution,
    16, 75, 120
  Eight Ways of Thinking of a, 79
  embodies the brand promise, 23,
    73, 75, 91, 119, 122, 146, 150
  essential competencies for a, 44
  focus on mission, core values and
    strategic objectives, 40
  intentional ways of being of a, 80

intuition and instinct, 20, 77
leads change rather than controls
    it, 151
maintains an awareness of world
    events that impact the business,
    30
make a decision with a strong
    inward compass, 137
noble and humble, 122
observations from interviews with, 82
the power of, 65–71
ritualizes ingenuity, 67
structure of the ways of, 45, 165
tailors decisions to fit the location
    and culture, 30
transforms knowledge about US
    markets to global markets, 30
ways of a, 73, 166
ways of thinking of, 74

leaders
    authentic, 88
    is a brand, 4, 10
    comfortable making hard
        decisions, 117
    compassionate, 35
    contemplative, 26
    effective are self-aware, 101
    focuses on building relationships, 90
    foundation of a, 10
    innovative, 31
    lack of trust in the, 11
    learn from one another, 15
    must foster innovation, 68
    organizational, 68
    shares expectations, 89
    significant challenges for, 46
    strategic, 41, 100
    trust their own good judgment,
        instincts, and intuition, 117
    a valuable tool for, 51
    way of thinking, 45, 61, 150
    who set the tone, 117
leadership
    balanced thinking, 32, 35
    capabilities, 4

challenges, 13, 50, 74, 78
characteristics and behaviors, 10,
    25, 40, 44, 73–4, 78–9, 91,
    133
collaborative approach, 53, 81
collaborative leadership, 16, 19,
    77, 118, 150
competencies, 24, 114
contemporary literature, 45
continuity plan, 29
in control, 13, 23, 45, 75, 77–8,
    137, 146, 149
and culture, 111
deeper dimensions of, 13
development of, 19, 95
development session, 46
dimensions, short-form and long-
    form, 145
effective, 99, 139
is far more intuitive than
    planned, 20
foundational aspects of, 65
it's time for a different paradigm,
    23, 164
mental maps about, 44
a new model of, 15, 164
Procter &Gamble, 7
paradoxical challenges of, 50
personal brand of, 74
questions about, 21
is a relationship, 150
as a relationship not a position,
    23, 75, 119–20, 146
resonant, 33, 163–4
scholars of, 16
self-assessment and scores, 147–8
is situational, 101
solid model, 147
spreading authority, 95
style, 10, 66, 73–4, 112, 142
team opportunities, 37
thinking about leadership from
    the inside out, 91
vision, 55
learning from mentors through The
    Eight Ways of Thinking, 117

Lechleiter, John, 29, 31, 65, 95, 106, 108, 120, 123, 126–7, 129, 134, 140
listening
active, 39, 88, 112
art of, the, 89
critical, 118
living organization, 15, 21, 38, 45, 50–1, 55, 56–7, 61, 74, 79, 118–19, 143, 149, 163–6

martial arts
material, 52, 80
spiritual, 54
and T'ai Chi, 69
Mazza, Ellen, 60
McDonald, Bob, 26, 40, 46, 69, 82, 87, 92, 106, 110, 121–2, 133, 136
mission
achieving the, 10
drives the numbers, 23, 76, 92, 119, 124, 146
elements, 69
fulfilling the, 90
institutionally-distinct, 92
internal values of, 137, 144
purpose and, 18, 76, 124
statement, 28, 94, 125
understand the, 129
versus market, 45
and vision, 32, 95
mistakes
admit, 17
owning up to, 123
personally ambitious versus the organization, 121
networks
building, 94
can encourage diversity, 152
change the structure of an organization, 152
versus hierarchies, 45
of influence, 20, 77, 127
purpose-driven, 152
use of, 152

Nieman, Harry, 30–1, 33, 64, 90, 94
objectives
business, 32
clear, 43
define the, 95
key, 40
organizational, 44
principle, 125
optimism
healthy, 67
respect for possibilities, 64, 68
organization
brand promise, 91
complex, 106
critical success factors, 38
decentralized, 31
diverse, 144
framework for, 46
growth cycle, 39
high-trust, 65
how an organization survives, 23
mission statement, 28
objectives, 29
survival, 29, 63, 166
unwieldy, 67
organizational
capabilities and competencies, 7, 21
challenges, 45, 51
competency, 58
different structures, 96
emerging structure, 152
failures, 97
issues, 30
mission, 93
resiliency, 44, 69
success, 33, 71, 154
values, 28, 157
ownership, sense of, 112, 132

PACE of Change Model, 41–3, 113
Pepper, John, 27, 31, 90, 124–5, 130, 132, 137
personality differences, 70

perspective
  broader, 134
  diverse, 99
  experiential, 74
  historical, 67
Phillips, Marla, 33, 98, 123, 128,
    132, 136
power
  balance and, 57–8
  circulate the, 49
  distributing, 52
  factor, 54, 81
  harnessing the, 17, 75
  intellectual, 79
  of leadership, the, 63, 166
  name of the game, the, 128
  sharing, 20, 30–1, 38, 44, 95
  side of the framework, 52, 105, 107
  together and, 55, 78
  will, 60
principles
  of Aikido, 80
  ethical, 90
  purpose-driven, 53
  stated, 64
  values and, 75, 122
Procter & Gamble, 3, 26–7, 31, 40,
    46, 63, 87, 90, 93, 101, 125,
    143–4
  leadership, 7
promise
  delivering on the, 9–10
  fulfilling, 6

Quality Dialogue Questions, 37, 66

real world
  challenges, 78
  constraints, 32
  experience, 153
  learning in the, 19
reflection
  and action, 51, 81
  and balance, 123
  function of, 140
  individual, 153–4

intentional, 25–7
  self-reflection, 82–3
  shared, 10
relationships
  building, 90, 120, 126
  constructive, 21, 61, 119, 149
  trusting, 143
  working, 111
Research Foundation for
    Leadership in Balance, 143
resiliency = change = infinity, 68
resilient organizations
  a balance between risk and
    tradition, 63
  are evolving organizations, 68
  intentional design for, 69
  model for, 64, 67, 70

Schroder, Jeff, 111
self-confidence
  enhance, 83
  lack of, 82
Senge, Peter, 143, 163, 167
Shazor, Marilyn, 27, 34, 95, 99
skepticism, intelligent, 67
strategic
  objectives, 31, 40
  perspective, 27, 44
strategic planning
  behaviors must be called upon to
    implement the plan, 41
  execution, 97
  methods, 96
  process, 100
strategies
  create better, 143
  execute the, 125
strategist, head of a, 74, 119
successful change initiatives, 39

T'ai Chi, 69
Tao, 82
teaching
  the art of, 19
  helping another person be all
    they can be, 130

teaching—*Continued*
  and leadership have a great deal
    in common, 19, 23, 77, 97,
    119, 129
thinking
  behaviors for, 87–100
  Eight Ways of Thinking, The,
    117–18
  influences the heart of a moral
    and ethical leader, 122
  a leader's ways of, 149–50
  new way of, 5, 135
  shift in, 59, 153
  short-term thinking, 124
  top-leadership-level, 147
  ways of, 132, 146, 151
Torbert, William R., 78
trust
  is always earned, 12
  builder of, 74, 119
  building, 87, 89, 122

  conveying, 130
  is important, 126
  low public trust in institutions
    today, 4
  Trust Audit, 64–6
  work environment, 27
Tzu, Sun, 52, 80
Ueshiba, Morihei, 53, 81
values
  ethical values, 17
  of mission and purpose, 137, 144
  personal, 28, 90
  a set of, 56, 61, 91
Vivek, Paul, 32
Washkewicz, Don, 26, 31, 33, 68,
    93, 117, 120
Welsh, Jack, 15
Wrigley, Jr., William, 38
Xavier University's Leadership
    Institute, 145, 147
Yin and yang, 58–9

About the Authors

Photo by Greg Rust

John F. Kucia is Administrative Vice President at Xavier University, USA. With 37 years as a practitioner of collaborative leadership in the fields of health care and higher education, Kucia has drawn upon his extensive experience to research this unique and unstudied topic.

Linda S. Gravett is Founder and Senior Partner of Gravett and Associates, an established management consulting agency, and

President and CEO of Just the Basics, Inc., an executive coaching and strategic planning firm for small companies and non-profits. Gravett is the author of one textbook, *HRM Ethics: Perspectives for a New Millennium*, and co-author of *Bridging the Generation Gap*, *Using Your Emotional Intelligence to Develop Others*, and *Just a Couple of Women Talkin'*.